WHAT IT TAKES TO PLAY FOR THE COUNTRY

FOREWORD BY **WAYNE SPRATFORD** SPORT SCIENTIST AT THE AUSTRALIAN BOARD OF CRICKET

NIKHIL JAIN

BLUEROSE PUBLISHERS
India | U.K.

Copyright © Nikhil Jain 2024

All rights reserved by author. No part of this publication may be reproduced, stored in a retrieval system or transmitted in any form or by any means, electronic, mechanical, photocopying, recording or otherwise, without the prior permission of the author. Although every precaution has been taken to verify the accuracy of the information contained herein, the publisher assumes no responsibility for any errors or omissions. No liability is assumed for damages that may result from the use of information contained within.

BlueRose Publishers takes no responsibility for any damages, losses, or liabilities that may arise from the use or misuse of the information, products, or services provided in this publication.

For permissions requests or inquiries regarding this publication, please contact:

BLUEROSE PUBLISHERS
www.BlueRoseONE.com
info@bluerosepublishers.com
+91 8882 898 898
+4407342408967

ISBN: 978-93-5989-910-7

Cover design: Shivam

First Edition: October 2024

Dedicated to:

The serious cricketer, child or adult, who wants to play for the country

GUARANTEE FROM AUTHOR:

If you find that upon reading the contents of this manual that you did not learn anything or did not get an accurate and precise idea of the skills one needs to gain to aim for national selection, and didn't gain a grasp of the what and why behind cricket such that you understand what to do and why you are doing it, then please email us on phd.cricket@gmail.com with your account details and we will give you a full refund of the price you paid for it minus postage cost. Any profit or proceed we received from your order will be refunded and returned in full.

USE OF THIS MANUAL:

Use this manual as a source of inspiration in your dreams of playing for the country. Take in and absorb all the lessons and insights regards playing quality cricket and try to really hone your cricketing powers before you go looking for and expect state or national selection. Familiarize yourself with the core as well as finer skills you will need to play a quality brand of cricket and don't be apprehensive about where you are going or where your cricketing journey is going to take you, but rather try to master the topics discussed within the book and practice with full focus and dedication. Don't look around you to see where you stand in front of other boys playing the game just yet. The book is intended to teach and explicitly outline what skills and abilities it will take to gain national selection for aspiring cricketers from all countries.

Playing for the Country:

Kohli, Warner or Gayle. Shall you be great and not just good. May you sail your ship to shore just like a seaman would.

Mind, body & spirit, the very makings and elements of a cricketer's periodic table. Whether the elements are there or not it is having the steel which scripts the fable.

Science and mathematics screams the endearing fan, and we were just hoping that you had a plan. Did you not listen to the coach and his wisdom, what happened to all those loose balls you absolutely missed them.

How you played the game is the means to the end, for they all hope it is not time to walk back to the pavillion my dear friend. And with 200 million onlookers before us, surely hard work and practice on our game will reap rewards, and may they be marvellous.

May you earn and wear the country's cap with pride and honour. After everything with our books is done and said, may you be mused by the finer points of cricket, and our books be read.

FOREWORD by 'Wayne Spratford'

Sport Scientist at Board of Cricket Australia & Sport Science researcher at University of Canberra, Australia

A topical guide which reaches out to the common man and depicts and defines what exactly you will need to do to gain national selection and reveals the intricacies of the game which matter most and which must be acquired to play for your country. The perfect introduction to the game of cricket and its many nuances, which discusses the important facets of cricket and the finer points one must have a grasp over in order to play a quality brand of cricket.

I fully support the author in his wish of *"giving every child and adult an equal and fair opportunity to play for the country"*, and believe the contents of the book to be the perfect starting point before one delves and embarks upon the journey of how to actually achieve one's end goal in cricket. The explanation and understanding of the game which the reader will acquire, in my eyes, is unrivalled and will have even the common man or layman mused by the facets and intricacies of cricket which are necessitated in international level cricket.

For the serious and already active cricketer, be it a child or an adult, the book offers many key takeaways and really does drill into the reader's conscious mind what is required in cricket and what is required to play the game for the country. Short yet elaborate, I believe the book is among the better books ever written on cricket and can be especially useful to the minnow nations who don't yet have a grip on the fundamentals or finer aspects of the sport and quality coaches to show them and guide them through the intricacies of the game.

DEDICATION

This book is dedicated to all of you serious cricketers out there who harbor hopes and foster ambitions to be a serious and accomplished cricketer, and aim for national selection. Cricket is not an easy sport and there is a lot to learn and there is a lot of mentoring and guidance which one must have in order to accomplish such a daring feat. The way we see it is that the serious cricketer should not only be coached and trained in the niche skills elite cricket involves, but be given an explicit outline and synopsis of each and every skill which he/she must master before one can embark on the difficult and arduous task of ultimately mastering these tasks and representing the nation. That is, one should be counselled in regards the specific skills necessary and it should be explicitly defined as to what is important and why to us cricketers aiming to lift their game whilst and even before one embarks on the challenging and onerous task of rising the ranks to play for the country!

We need to understand the what and the why before we begin work on the actual how and in cricket, something which is encumbered with a plethora of varying approaches, styles, techniques and processes or means, you could call it, can be of enormous benefit. Yes, that's right, in cricket there is not only a colossal amount of skill, dexterity and skill sets required but infinite and limitless ways of performing our roles and ultimately achieving our end goal – which is to either score runs or get wickets.

Cricket is a sport which encompasses many finer aspects and individual facets and which combined and in totality form what you could call a competent cricketer. That is, if we are to accomplish our end goal of simply being a great cricketer or improving our skills marginally or even fostering the hope of playing for the country, then the whole aggregate or total must be looked at fragment by fragment part by part and it's constituent elements must be delved into, studied and mastered individually and one by one in the most scrupulous and precise manner possible.

One must know what he has to do and why he has to do it before he can set about the exploration, campaign or task of actually doing it, which in this context is playing your cricket in the most precise, exact and proper way possible. There is more than meets the eye in cricket and there is a certain hidden science which is not obvious to the naked eye and it is this hidden science and the exact treatment of its comprising parts or fragments as an overall subject domain which we are here to offer you education in regards to and ultimately give you a clearer picture into the deeper science which proliferates and is manifests itself within this game called cricket.

This book will not only discuss the what and why but to some extent also go into the how, and is the perfect piece of reading for one who is serious about embarking upon the difficult passage
Or voyage which ensues whilst training to become the final finished product – a national level cricketer!

The book is primarily dedicated to the child, adolescent or teen and seeks to engrain within him/her, from a young age itself, what it takes to play at the highest international level and what exactly is required of you to do so in entirety and exactitude!

PREFACE

Cricket has from the very beginning been considered the great mental game and a game which started out as one played by the civilized and elite communities of England. However, actually possessing and having a grip over the complete science involved in the game was something which had to somewhat evolve, mature or emerge gradually and emerge gradually as the game gained more popularity, respect and worthy of being a valid past time or professionally contested sport.

In the modern era nothing is left to chance and serious students of the game now have access to one-to-one coaching and being part of specialized coaching clinics or academies as well as a vast amount of literature on the subject aimed at imparting and transferring key scientific concepts important in cricket. This book does exactly that and does so to the utmost standard of impeccability and exquisiteness and is what we would like to call the best source of formative guidance offered within the modern era of cricket, which is the era of the deployment of scientific and technological advances which knows not what the meaning of the word *'impossible'* is.

When technology and science can fly 3 people to the moon and when technology can explore the deepest depths of the ocean and find the ruins of the Titanic and when technology can build and engineer robots, then why would the game of cricket not progress in parallel with this new era of technological upscaling. An era which has revolutionized the world and the way we live within it and an era where there have been rapid advances in how science and scientific understanding is here to save the day and is enshrouded by the ethos that nothing is impossible for man and mankind's pursuits of understanding, building and improving the world he lives in. This ethos or rationality that science is here to save the day and that science can achieve anything is what the common man now needs to be accepting of and embellish, and be cautious to not get left behind in this great era of science and a technologically booming world.

It is this very science, the science necessitated in a game of cricket that is, which we through this book wish to offer and impart upon you the reader such that you don't get left behind and play your cricket in an unguided, imprecise and unscientific manner, and that too in a world where professional sports are highly lucrative and competitive and athletes are known to use any means and ways known to compete and achieve the end result – victory!

The means to the ends and how you played the game is what matters and decides victory or defeat in sports and this book is especially dedicated to teaching you the full science and scientific cruxes upon which cricket is based around, and not allow you to get left behind and be deprived of having a scientific answer to a scientific problem. As we said, batting is a pure science and performances in most if not all sports is somewhat a matter of scientific rigor and scientific and rigorous coaching as opposed to being an art form requiring any form of artistic aptitude per say.

Further, cricket is perhaps one of the most mental and scientific sports of all and we are here to give you the full and entire rundown on every piece of science involved in developing your cricketing prowess and playing for the country. Just read and be patient! We know your time is valuable and reading can sometimes become encumbering and difficult.

So simply have faith and not only read this book for the what and why but ensure you read our other books for the deeper understanding of the how!

INTRODUCTION

It is when we are acquainted with the what we have to do and understand precisely why we have to do it in a certain manner or way that we can give ourselves a more spirited impetus and drive to undertake the task of actually doing it and performing it properly. Like we said, cricket is not only a mental game and one based around scientific cruxes, but one which is considered a rather large subject domain in regards to specific, individual and key skills required for its successful execution.

There are many things which matter in cricket and there are many things, which if done right, can drastically improve your cricket, and there are many things which if NOT done right can hinder, hamper or impede your cricket significantly also. Cricket truly is a very scientific and complex sport and one which is full of little nuances, finer points and mental thought processes which can make or break your hopes of rising the ranks and making a career out of cricket.

This book is not merely for fun or to be read at one's own leisure but a book which absolutely **MUST** be read if you are serious about your cricket and serious about playing for the country. You must take the time and care and afford of yourself the time taken for the necessary training and undergo a formative process of an acceptable quality if you are to master and perfect your game and go on to play for the country. This book is the perfect investment of your time and is a highly intensive work of applied science where we show you in minute detail how the science can actually improve your cricket.

Playing for the country is not a joke. It is highly competitive and demands of you to be at the top of your game and partaken and passed certain milestones and checks in regards to technical competence in either bowling or batting, whichever one you happen to be. There is no such thing as sneaking in through the back door when we talk about international level cricket and there is no short cut – you must have actually honed and practiced your skills to the utmost level of rigor and nicety to be in contention for national selection.

There is no such thing as being strong because your neighbors are weak in cricket for it is a competitive sport and everybody is following the same human instinct which equates to the fact that we all want to play for the country. This urge to aspire for national selection facilitates the standard of any nation's cricket to gradually become higher and higher – this is what leads to not being able to call ourselves strong just because our neighbors are weak because there is no longer a weak neighbor. If we want to win and win selection we must develop our strengths sincerely and wholeheartedly – that is what will give you the nerve to call yourself strong!

So do not take the task ahead of you lightly! You must actually develop, grow and hone your powers if you are to be in contention for national selection, as millions are trying to do the same and there is no such thing as a weak neighbor, especially for all those from the major cricket playing countries where selection is highly competitive. For the major test playing nations the fact remains and cannot be ignored that you will be judged and weighed up based upon the actual mastery and skill level you have acquired on the game of cricket, and not just on the basis that "well there is a position to fill on the team and lets just give it to him because there is no one better". For the major cricket playing nations there almost always is someone better – that is the difference.

For cricket is already a difficult sport to master and if you come from one of the major test playing nations then there will be many participants and enthusiastic athletes competing for a select few positions in either the state or national level squads, and it is only through actual mastery of the discipline of batting and bowling which will see you go on and go ahead to play national levels.

Like we said, cricket has a vast array of skill sets and possibilities and options and is one sport where you need to be alert of what exactly you are trying to do and why exactly you are trying to do it, as cricket is a pure science and **NOT** an art or any type of an art form. It is a game which more so relies upon a player being precise, particular and decisive in regard how he is going to achieve the end result – which is runs and wickets.

This book mainly concentrates on the what and why and elucidates to you what you have to do in cricket and why as opposed to going into elaborate detail as to the exact how you are going to do it. For this, the deeper understanding of the how that is, you will have to read our other specialized coaching manuals. In this book we simply make you aware of what skills you will need to acquire for contentions for national selection and why they are important. Through this book we are simply trying to inculcate within you and your sub-conscious mind aspects and facets to cricket which you will need to gain a complete mastery over, if you are to actually go ahead and be picked for the country, and do so in the most brief and comprehendible fashion possible and with minimal verbosity.

This book is not a comprehensive guide as to exactly how to do something – this is what has been discussed at great depth within our other books. The purpose of this book is to merely make you aware of the little things it will take a bigger concentration on in order to raise your game sufficiently enough to be a contender and a chance for national selection.

Table of Contents

SECTION I: BATTING

Chapter 1 – Pick the length..1

Chapter 2 –Playing the length ball....................................8

Chapter 3 - Adjustment of Technique & Back lift................ 16

Chapter 4 – Primary Versus Peripheral vision......................21

Chapter 5 - Visual acuity: Deciphering amongst 4 layers……...26

Chapter 6 – Playing the erratically swinging ball………....…32

Chapter 7 - Batting when there is no deviation....................35

Chapter 8 – Finding the gaps in the field..........................37

Chapter 9 – Hitting across the line..................................40

Chapter 10 – Lofting the ball over the infield.....................44

Chapter 11 – Building an innings - play defense at the start......45

Chapter 12 – Estimating & determining the z-box ASAP……..49

Chapter 13 – Maximising scoring from within the c-box………55

Chapter 14 – Batting technique………………………….....57

Chapter 15 – Choosing your stroke……………………….65

Chapter 16 – Handling pressure………………………......69

Chapter 17 – The 2 stages of batting development……….….71

Chapter 18 – The parallel vs sequential method of picking line……………………………………………………..76

Chapter 19 – Use that bottom hand…………………….81

SECTION II: FAST BOWLING

Chapter 20 – Becoming the spearhead of the fast bowling attack……………………………………………………………..87

SECTION III: SPIN BOWLING

Chapter 21 – Can YOU be a great spin bowler…………………...91

SECTION IV: FIELDING

Chapter 22 – Becoming a good fielder…………………………..93

SECTION V: CAPTAINCY

Chapter 23 – Captaincy is SO important…..………..…………...97

SECTION VI: WICKET KEEPING

Chapter 24 – becoming a competent Wicket keeper……..…….103

SECTION VII: THE PROFESSIONAL CRICKETER

Chapter 25 – Batting at the highest level……..………………….105

Chapter 26 – bowling at the highest level……..………………..111

Chapter 27 – Test cricket vs one day cricket mode……………114

A NOTE BY THE AUTHOR……………………..………..121

CHAPTER 1
PICK THE LENGTH:

Picking the length essentially equates to the fact that the batsman is trying to foresee or predict the exact shape and direction the ball is about to take. First he must observe the height from which the ball is being released; then he must predict the projected ball-pitch contact the ball is about to take, or simply put, where on the pitch the ball is anticipated to land. Then lastly he must deduce from these two parameters exactly how high the ball is going to bounce. So it is **NOT** just seeing where on the pitch the ball is about to land – it is more than that! It is about deducing where the ball will be by the time it comes closer and closer to your body and bat and relies upon a certain science in order to be done – to pick the length that is.

Firstly, we must do what we call a vector reading or a vector analysis which essentially involves seeing from what height the ball is being released from and watching hard as to what the position of the ball is by something called a *'Z-Point'*. Once this is known the ball-pitch interception point can be deduced and how high the ball will bounce can be deduced. This is the process which in cricket is known as 'picking the length', and has now been explicitly explained to you.

We can't just wait and watch the ball and wait to visualize what the shape of the ball will be and ascertain where the ball will be in proximity to our bodies and bat at the very last moment, but rather, **MUST** know this information well and well before the ball journeys down the pitch and must have the aptitude or aptness to actually predict and visualize in our minds what exactly the shape of the ball will be by a certain time known as the Z-Point.

One more piece of science is also intertwined with the whole concept of picking the length for a batsman and that is Euclid's law of angle of reflection is always equal to the angle of incidence. Inspect the following diagrams for a better depiction of what exactly it takes to *'pick the length'*.

Diagram 1: The z-point:

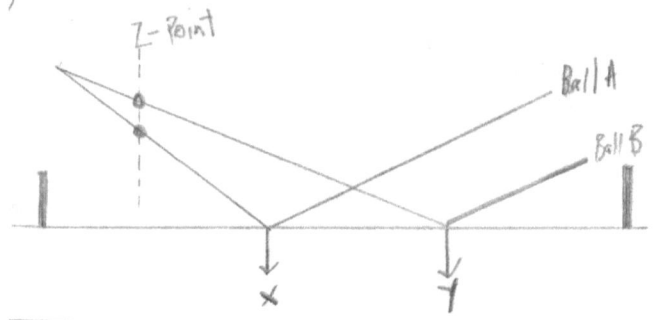

So we see that ball A bounces more and ball B bounces less and that the position of the ball s per by the z-point is different. By observing the position and behavior of the ball by z-point, we can easily make out that one ball will bounce at ball-pitch interception point X and the other at ball-pitch interception point Y. This is all it takes to pick the length and pick it the way the professionals do – to watch the ball hard until z-point that is.

Upon observing the ball's position in the air by z-point, we then rely on Euclid's law of angle of incidence equals angle of reflection, and can easily track and visualize the exact path and shape the ball will take in advance. Inspect the following diagram.

Diagram 2: Euclid's law of angle of reflection equals angle of incidence

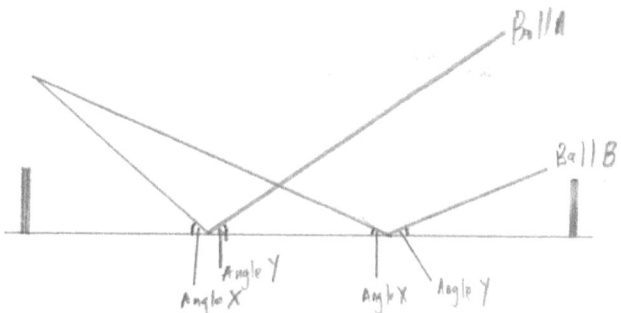

So we see on the diagram that angle X is equal to angle Y for both balls A and B. This is what is known as Euclid's law in motion and is of enormous importance for you batsmen out there who must get in to position early as well as pick the shape and profile of the ball early enough to play a forceful and run yielding stroke.

This law comes from the subject of optics from physics and has been proven to be true for thousands of years and across many industrial applications as well as many ball sports – so why not cricket! In fact cricket is one sport where Euclid's law is of absolute critical importance and in conjunction with vector forces forces is something which one could say is the very core and fundamental of batting per say. There is no room for batsmen who don't know how to pick the length the scientific way and the way we have just shown you, and you simply will **NOT** develop the game and power and placement in your shots to play for the country unless and until you start seeing and closely watching the ball's position by z-point and be able to deduce the exact shape the ball is going to take!

So soon after the ball has been released, say 1 – 2 meters, we are required to project, predict and foresee the exact shape the ball is about to take and get ourselves into position early and early enough to play the right shot and the one which yields the most runs. Inspect the following diagram for this depiction of the z-point which represents the time by which the ensuing length of the ball **CAN** and **SHOULD** be accurately determined. This point is anywhere between 1 meter from the ball's point of release to about 2 meters from the ball's point of release, and is not as such a point exactly but a rough zone or time frame by which the ball's final shape should be ascertained.

Diagram 3: The position of the Z-point or Z-zone

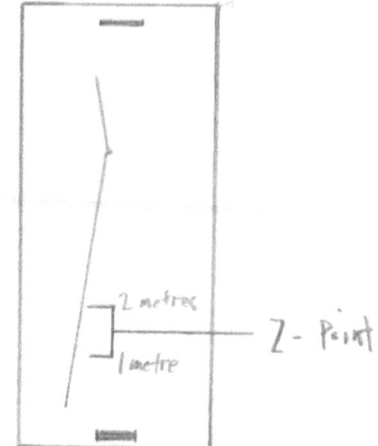

So picking the length according to the method aforementioned and depicted is one of the most important skills for a batsman and separates the goods from the greats and is one causative factor in deciding whether or not you will go onto play for the country or not!

There is more to picking the length than just determining and visualizing the actual length the ball will bounce at – it is a little more multiplex than that! Inspect the following diagram:

Diagram 4: Point of release must be considered before we can 'pick the length'

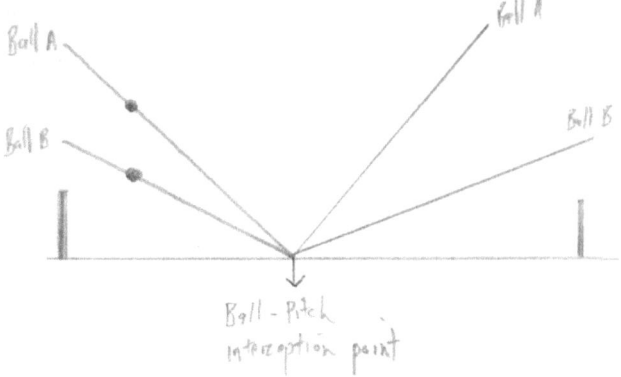

So we see that Ball A and Ball B land at the same spot – that's is, they both have the same *'ball-pitch interception point'!* So shouldn't the shape of the ball be the same and haven't I now successfully done what is called *'picking the length'?* well, the answer is no! You see in the diagram that the shape and bounce of the ball is vastly different despite both balls pitching at the sme length. Well we haven't considered the ensuing height or release point the ball is coming from and therefore **HAVE NOT** succeeded in picking the length. A vector has 2 scalars, which are magnitude and direction. Ball A and Ball B have the same magnitude but different directions. This is because Ball A is coming from different point or position and ultimately has a different direction and therefore the to deliveries both ball A and ball B are **NOT** the same vector. The two scalars of both balls is the same, in that being the force put on the ball , however, the direction scalar is different for both balls, hence resulting in a ball which, yes, pitches at the same length but has a different shape or *'resultant vector'* as we call it.

So this is what is referred to in cricket as picking the length. We must pick the 2 scalar quantities which ultimately form to be a vector. This is basically Euclidian physics and specifically his law of angle of reflection is **ALWAYS** equal to the angle of incidence. So if we know the bowler is short we can immediately deduce that no matter what the ball-pitch intercept point is, that the ball will **NOT** bounce as much. Similarly if the bowler is taller we can automatically deduce that where ever it bounces on the pitch, it will bounce slightly higher.

Don't be overwhelmed or confused by the technical jargon and pragmatism used to explain to you what exactly the science behind picking the length is. It is really very simple. The taller the bowler the more bounce and the shorter the bowler the less bounce. The higher the angle of incidence the higher the angle of reflection.

So you now know that there are a few metrics involved in picking the ball's length or in scientific jargon the ball's vector. Try to treat any given delivery in cricket as a vector and really concentrate on what its two constituent scalar quantities are, which is basically the height of the bowler and what position the ball will be released from **AND** the interception point or length the bowler is trying to pitch or land the ball at. This can be known, by some if not most batsman, well in advance and the ball-pitch interception point combined with what height the ball is coming from can easily be used to deduce the shape and bounce of the ball well in advance – say the two bolded circles in the previous diagram.

You now know how to pick the length – congratulations, and may it be an integral part of your batting and help you dominate the bowling and deduce or predict the ball's path and shape well in advance –just like the batsman who play for the country do!

This point by which we predict the vector on the ball is depicted as the two shaded balls in the diagram and it is by this point by which the batsman effectively predicts the ball-pitch interception point and thereafter the amount of bounce the ball will take.

This is called *'vector analysis'* in science and in cricket is simply called just *'picking the length'*.

Cricket and batting is something which is best done step by step or sequentially, and is best executed by performing and following each instruction in a linear and step by step fashion. So first determine the height of the bowler, which is fixed and is the first thing which we notice; then carefully watch where the ball's position in the air is by z-point; then deduce the *'ball-pitch interception point'*, then deduce the how high the bll is going to bounce, and then decide on what stroke or strokes are possible and which one you must play to find the gap.

Chapter 2
Playing the length ball:

There is more than meets the eye to playing the length ball and combined with the fact no two bowlers are of identical height and no two pitches have the same bounciness in them, the playing of the length ball involves a certain science to be brought to the table. There is something called the *'z-box'* which represents deliveries of a good line **AND** length, and is considered that particular ball which is in that perfect accurate and hard to score off zone. The length ball simply implies any delivery which is neither short **OR** full, and usually must be played with a sound, stable and solid defensive stroke. Inspect the following diagram for how the z-box is calculated.

Diagram 5: corridor of uncertainty

The corridor of uncertainty basically pertains to that accurate and nagging line which makes scoring for the batsman difficult. It starts around middle stump and extends to the off side by about 1 to 1.25 feet. Next we have what we call the length of uncertainty and represents those deliveries which are neither short enough nor full enough for the batsman to play a forceful attacking stroke. Inspect the following diagram:

Diagram 6: Length of uncertainty

Diagram 7: the good line **AND** length ball

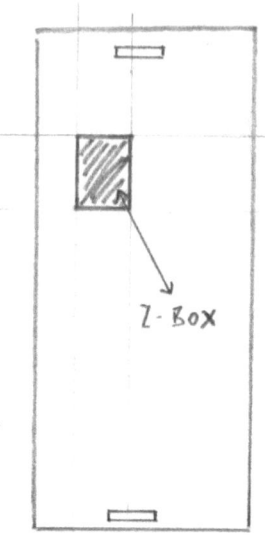

It is this little box where the two parameters of line **AND** length and their shaded areas are mutually inclusive, which defines what is a good ball and what is not! We call this the Z-box. So now we know what a good length ball is, how it is determined and where on the pitch it actually lies. Now for the part where we actually play such a delivery.

Again we use Euclid's law to forecast whether the ball will land within the *'z-box'* and whether or not any particular delivery will classify as a length ball or not. If we do anticipate the ball will be good and accurate in terms of length and **WILL** land within the z-box, then we have two options – to play our defensive stroke off the front foot **OR** to play our defensive shot of the back foot.

There is a certain rule or law which ultimately decides this. Inspect the following diagram:

Diagram 8: playing length ball off front foot or back foot

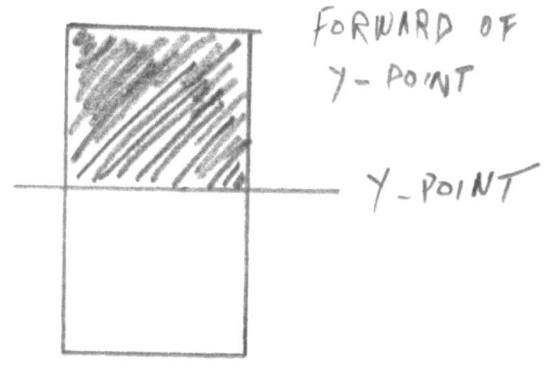

So you see the z-box, which by now you know represents the good length ball, as being divided into 2 zones – one is forward of the Y-point and one is backward of the Y-point. The Y-point simply represents that ball which is on that absolutely perfect length that scoring off this delivery is just humanly impossible. The z-box usually is about 6-8 balls in length and 3-4 balls in width, and as you can see is divided into two sections. The section which is shaded **ALWAYS MUST** be played off **FRONT FOOT** and the section which is unshaded can be played off EITHER front OR backfoot. It is just too dangerous and an impediment to our wicket to play the relatively pitched or full accurate ball off the back foot – we must **ALWAYS** play this ball off front foot.

A very critical and precarious aspect to playing the length ball pertains to the metrics of height of the bowler and the bounce or lack thereof in the pitch. Now that you know what the z-box is, we can begin teaching you how these two metrics affect and decide how you are to play the length ball.

Yes, the height of the bowler and the bounciness or lack thereof in the pitch actually **SHIFTS** where your z-box will be on the pitch and what constitutes a length ball and what does not! This is explained in depth within our book about Bradman and playing the length ball so we are only going to keep it brief. Inspect the below diagram:

Diagram 9: how length ball changes when bowler is taller

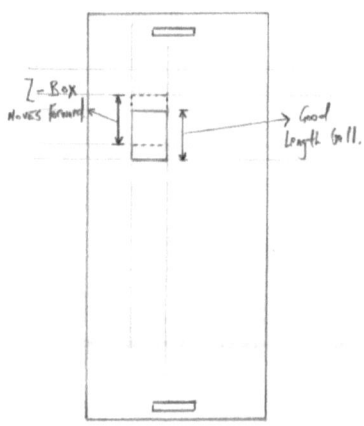

Because the bowler is taller he is getting the ball to bounce and steeple off a relatively fuller length and the conventional drive shot **CANNOT** be played. Similarly, because the bowler is taller and getting increased bounce a ball which would ordinarily be an accurate length is now short of a length and can be played off back foot and even cut or pulled.

Diagram 10: how length ball changes when bowler is shorter

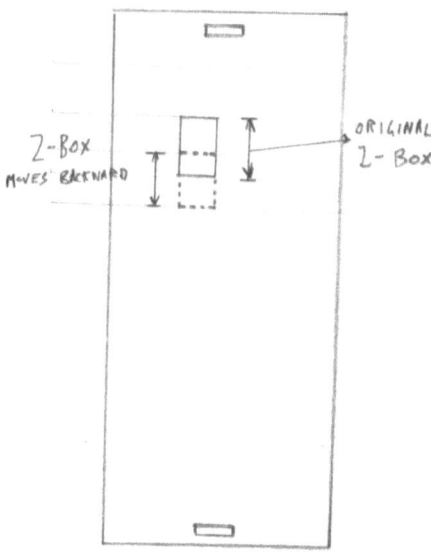

What was before a good length ball is now at a driving length and what was before a considered a short ball is no longer a short ball but because the bowler is shorter and generating less bounce, is now within a good accurate ball zone.

A similar thing happens when the pitch is either playing more bouncy or playing low and slow. Inspect the following diagram:

Diagram 11: how the length ball changes when pitch is keeping low

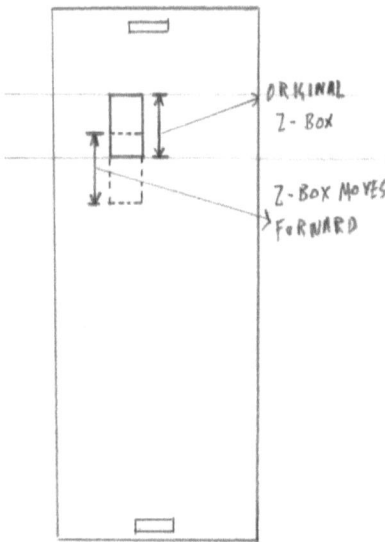

Because the pitch is keeping low a ball which would ordinarily be considered short is now in that good length zone, and a ball which would be considered accurate is now full enough to drive.

In a nutshell it all equates to this and the reason you have been doing all this reading is to acknowledge and use this little theory of batting, which is considered very much a revered secret of the game and is not shared by coaches you are paying to teach you, and that is:

"When the pitch is playing fast and bouncy, the ball pitches slightly full and appears to be at driving length, but it is NOT. It

is about to bounce steeply and should be treated with a forward defense or shot off the back foot even"

"When the pitch is playing slow and low, the ball pitches slightly short and appears to be a short ball and short of a length, but it is NOT. It is about to keep low once upon hitting the pitch, and should be treated with a forward defense or a drive"

So this is the hidden science behind playing the length ball. As you can appreciate, it simply embellishes the fact that the z-box shifts and moves either forward or back depending on the height of the bowler and the bounciness or lack thereof in the pitch. You now know when exactly and the circumstances wherein this happens.

To play for the country, you must know when and why and by how much the z-box moves forward or back and this understanding is essentially what you need to know in regards playing the length ball to perfection and just as a seasoned professional would.

Chapter 3
Adjustment of Technique and Backlift:

There are many back-lift positions deployed by the serious and accomplished batter. These are all determined by the amount of lateral ways movement the bowler is generating. As the saying goes *'play in the V early'*, this is not said for no reason! It is when we begin playing higher level cricket where no two pitches are identical **AND** the bowlers are almost always extracting lateral ways movement that we need to adjust our technique and back-lift accordingly. Because the bowler is toiling hard to get the outside edge via the outswinger as well as get the inswinger to sneak through the gate, a certain adjustment in bodily movement and mental thought process **MUST** be brought to the table.

To prevent the outside from happening and subsequently carrying through to the slips cordon for a caught behind, we deploy what is known as a *'straight back-lift and straight follow through'*, and this is most critical at the start of the innings when we don't know what the bowler is capable of and what not. Yes, the aim of any batter is to score freely and hit boundaries and play forceful shots, but he must go through his little sighter period first before he knows how to choose which ball to hit. Just in case the ball is swinging erratically, we must play straight, play with soft hands and let the ball come to you and present the full face of the bat to a ball which may potentially swing and deviate late, and whats more to some extent be in cautionary and defensive mode.

The backlift which generates maximum batspeed and power comes from about 2nd to 3rd slip, but if we adopt this back-lift early we give our wicket away cheaply to the good accurate ball which swings. To protect ourselves from this barrage of swinging deliveries the bowler is going to subject you to **CAN** be counteracted by simply adjusting your backlift. If you can bring your bat down from dead straight and follow through dead straight, then you have every chance of negating the imnpact the swinging ball has and can substantially reduce your chances of getting the edge and getting the caught behind. If you play with soft hands and play the ball late you **CAN** and **WILL** successfully negate the absolutely dire impact the swinging ball can have at the start of a batsman's innings.

Once we gauge how much lateral ways movement or swing the bowler is capable of getting we can then bring our back-lift around to 2nd or 3rd slip, but until then we must protect our wicket and protect ourselves from the out-swinger **AND** in-swinger whilst we are fresh to the crease and are not yet warm.

This is the very reasoning for playing in the *'V'* early – so we don't get the outside edge which carries through to the slip cordon and is something every great batsman possesses as an innings building skill. By adjusting our technique and back-lift early in the innings we can afford ourselves the ability to build an innings through patience, composure and restraint and give ourselves the best chance of getting on top of the pitch and bowling and going on to make a century.

We also should endeavor to get our body behind the line of the ball and if the ball deviates from its initial line, because we have our body behind the ball, we can better deal with and minimize the implications of inaptly dealing with the moving ball. By getting our body behind the line in defense, we essentially try to play the ball as close to the body as is possible given the ball will deviate by an unknown amount or quantity.

We must also, especially at the start of the innings, keep our elbow high and keep our bat and pad close together. By keeping a high elbow and using soft hands and playing the ball late and letting the ball come to us we can better negate the dire impact the swinging ball can have on our hopes of surviving the sighter period and going on to make a score for ourselves.

There is a certain technical expertise and mental process demanded of you as a batsman if your are to accurately gauge the pitch and bowling whilst keeping your wicket intact, and ultimately go on to make a score. One of the critical facets of gaining expertise in the act of batting is related to the visionary process and how and when to adjust it. This is what we will be talking about in the next chapter.

So remember, to play straight and follow through straight and present the full face of the bat whilst fresh to the crease and let the ball come to you and do something which is called *'make the bowler bowl to you'*. Be weary of the pitched up one which swings. If the bsll is too short, wide or full then definitely play your full attacking shot, but if it is accurate or even semi-accurate just play straight and with soft hands and make the bowler bowl to you. Inspect the following diagram for the various backlift positions and which one you need to follow in order to survive your sighter period and be successful in going on to make a century.

Diagram 12: various backlift positions and various follow thru

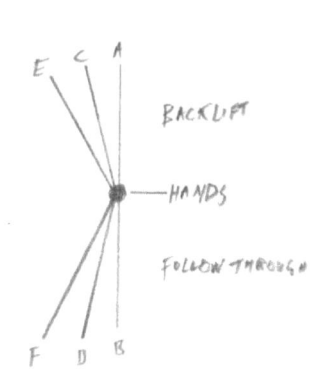

So position A – B is what we want at the start of our innings and is perfect for negating the impact the swinging ball can have on our wicket. Also we should adopt a less cocked backlift position also – this also aids in preventing the edge, if it does happen, from carrying through to slips. Inspect the following diagram for a depiction of this.

Diagram 13: less cocked back lift during start of innings

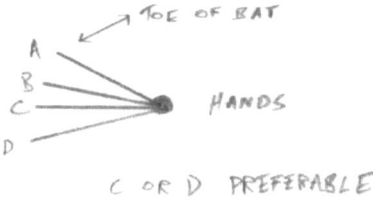

So there are certain fine tunings which we must make if we are to be a successful and triumphant batsman at the highest level of cricket. These are all things which matter in high level cricket played on turf and with a shiny red hard cricket ball under the pressure and expectations of a country on your shoulders, and we are foolish to ignore such finer details when we are aiming for the consistent performances which ultimately lead to state or national selection.

CHAPTER 4
PRIMARY VERSUS PERIPHERAL VISION:

This is one idea and phenomenon which is used in almost all sports. Primary vision refers to what you are going to focus on and devote all your mental and visual energies towards, and peripheral or secondary vision what you are going to, yes, see but not make the center of attention and actually be looking out for it sacrilegiously. What is this phenomenon's implications to us a s batsman? Well it is of enormous benefit and it is a visualization technique deployed by all good batsman.

Its application in cricket is relatively straight forward and easy to teach. While you are fresh to the crease and are just getting warmed up and getting used to the pitch and the bowler, we want to protect our wicket from the good accurate ball and devote **ALL** of our visual, seeing and mental energy to the possibility of getting *'a good one'* and getting out; and only leave part of our vision open to the loose ball. That is, we focus our primary vision on the good accurate length ball zone and leave only a fragment of our attention to the loose ball which may need to be punished.

We are referring to the way we register the ball's shape in our minds and the way in which we distribute or allocate our seeing energy. It has nothing to do with seeing straight out of the eye in a straight and focused manner opposed to seeing out the corner of the eye and concentrating on anything which is in sight from the side of our eyes! It is a mental distribution of energy and focusing technique we are referring to - by talking about primary and peripheral vision that is. In the start of our innings we are weary and apprehensive about keeping our wicket intact and surviving the good length and line accurate ball and it is now we really have to focus and watch hard on that area on the pitch which the good length accurate ball will land and be vigilant or alert as to negotiating anything which lands within the z-box. Almost like a tunnel eye vision or a selective hearing, we must be fully alert, aware and on the watch out for the good length ball and don't worry about anything else. In effect, we are being prudent and cautious about anything which is of a good line and length and only allowing a very small portion of our conscious visual energy for the bad length and line ball.[1]

This usually continues for at least 5-7 balls until the batter has a feel for the pitch and the bowling, focusing our visual energy on the good accurate ball that is, and relapses to what we call the default way in which we see, judge and process the ball. The batsman is there to score runs and he must focus his energy on the bad line and length ball and do what he has been sent out there to do, but he first must get played in and protect himself from the good accurate ball in the beginning if he is to even stay at the crease and not get packing back to the pavilions.

So, yes, to conduct a mature and meticulous brand of batting, we must make this adjustment to the way we are seeing the ball and whether we are seeing the ball through the lenses of caution and wariness **OR** whether we are seeing the ball through the lenses of boldness and tenacity, and make this adjustment to the visual process deployed especially whilst starting and building an innings. Like we said the batsman's job is to get runs thick and fast and that he must start focusing his primary vision on the loose

---

[1] Even whilst getting a sighter and focussing primary vision on good accurate ball whilst keeping peripheral vision open to loose ball, we can still play the pull shot and the drive whilst we are conducting our sighter period!

and inaccurate delivery, so this need not last beyond the time taken to get a *'sighter'* or get played in and we can soon start focusing our primary vision on the loose or even semi loose ball and start striking the ball hard, and only focus our secondary vision and keep a lookout for the good accurate ball. The best way to do this is what is called the *'L-Box'* method, the method we use to protect ourselves at the start of an innings yet still keep a peephole open to the loose ball. Inspect the diagram below.

Diagram 14: Bad length **AND** line (L-Box method)

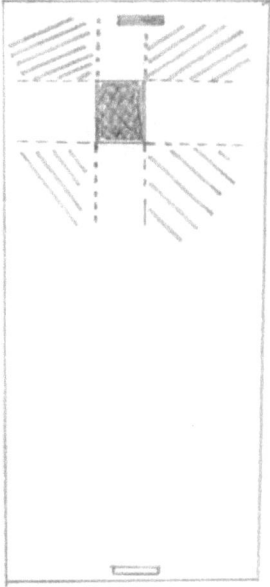

So the z-box which is shaded in bold is **ALL** we are trying to see and focus our visual energy and attention towards – balls of a good line **AND** length that is. The areas shaded in diagonal lines represents those balls witch lie within the bad length **AND** line zone and what we must keep our peripheral or secondary vision open to – even whilst we are getting a sighter.[2]

There are 3 layers or visual necessitations whilst batting and getting a sighter which centre around how exactly and when exactly to control and focus your primary vison. The 1st involves having almost a tunnel vision and only focusing on those balls which lie within that area called the corridor of uncertainty. Inspect the below diagram:

Diagram 15: primary vision focused on the corridor of uncertainty

We zone in and focus on anything landing within the corridor of uncertainty and nothing else. We focus our primary vision on this zone and do **NOT** play a stroke to anything outside of this zone. This is so we get an idea of how much swing the bowler is getting and need not last more than 3 balls. We then expand our horizons

---

[2] The L-box MUST be followed strictly at the start of your innings, however there are a few shots which you can play comfortably whilst still focussing your entire energy and attention to the z-box. These are the drive and the pull shot!

and start striking at those balls which are of a bad length **AND** line. This was depicted earlier by the L-box diagram prior. We are now still focusing our primary vision on the good accurate ball zone, but have now opened the shoulders a little and are now playing balls of a bad length **AND** line. Inspect the diagram below

<u>Diagram 16:</u> primary vision focused on good length ball whilst peripheral vision open to the bad length **AND** line ball

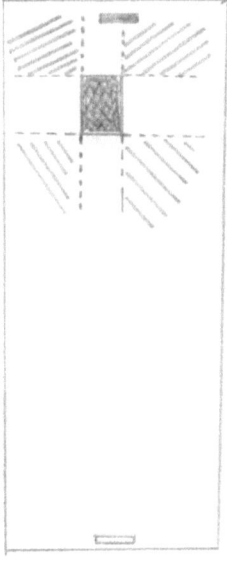

Chapter 5
VISUAL ACCUITY – DECIPHERING AMONG 4 LAYERS:

Vision and visual acuity and a sound, stable and error-free approach or process of seeing the ball is everything in cricket. Knowing which ball is loose and which ball is not, or knowing which balls to attack at and which to defend under varies circumstances and the way in which we focus our minds and visual energy, all comes down to this thing called the 4 layers of visual layers in batting. There are 3 z-boxes which represent the accurate ball and then there is this thing called the c-box which decides what balls are punishable and must be put away or scored from. Inspect the following diagram:

Diagram 17: The 4 layers of visual acuity in batting

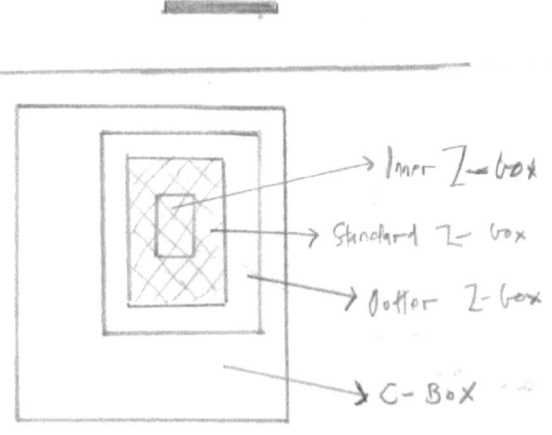

So we see there are 3 z-boxes and one c-box. What do they mean, what do they represent and why are they important? We will explain!

The standard z-box as you can see on the diagram represents those deliveries which would be considered accurate and treated with caution and circumspection and with a sound defensive shot. But what happens when we either have gotten our eye in and settled and played in? what do we do then? Well, we simply reduce the size of the z-box, which represents those balls which will be treated as accurate and with caution and anything outside of it with contempt and disdain.

Now balls which would be within the standard z-box range are in the loose to semi loose portion or range, and can subsequently by treated with an attacking shot. The outer z-box is when we are not warmed up, are not seeing the ball well **OR** if the bowler is getting too much lateral ways movement. Next we see the c-box – it stands for concentration-box. The c-box represents any ball which is not within the z-box or good accurate ball range and **CAN** and **SHOULD** be punished with a boundary hitting stroke or at least a 2 or a 3. We call it the concentration box because we really need to concentrate hard in regards to how we are going to hit it, where we are going to hit it and how we are going to maximize scoring opportunities off of it and is a zone on the pitch which really puts the batter under pressure as to how he is going to deal with it and choose among the plethora of stroke making options which lie before him, and pick the right one according to which yields the most runs and where the gap in the field is – this is why we call it the c-box or concentration box as the batsman is under supreme pressure to score big off anything outside of your inner z-box.

Diagram 18: depiction of c-box when batter is in form

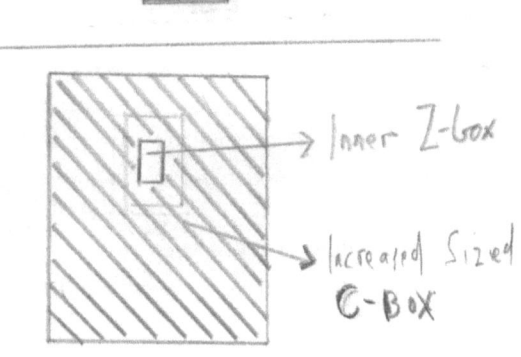

So now we have got our eye in and are seeing the ball well and have now reduced the size of our z-box to what is now an inner z-box. This effectively means the batsman is only playing defense if the ball lands within inner z-box and are really on the prowl as to scoring big off of anything outside of it and has now increased the size of the c-box – allowing him numerous more scoring stroke opportunities. What would happen if the ball was swinging too much and you are really having a bad day and are not warmed up yet or are struggling to see the ball? You would simply increase the size of the z-box and be more circumspect and cautious about deliveries which are now landing within a larger sized z-box. See diagram 17 below

This model to stroke selection is far superior to the simple section chart which is offered by so many cricket schools as it expositions and reveals each mental thought process and physical movement required in a step by step linear fashion. Section charts are like being told to buy a gun and shoot as many rabbits as you can. How do you know which gun to buy and which geographic area you must go to and whether to go at night or day and what is the technique for actually luring a rabbit to within shooting proximity or range. These all require instructions which must be provided in a linear and exact manner. The same goes for batting! We cant just give somebody a bat and say succeed and get a century! There are millions of factors and variables which must be conveyed and taught to the batsman before he can successfully perform his job of getting runs. Section charts are a sub-optimal method and means by which to teach stroke selection. You **MUST** follow these instructions and blocks of linear code which we have devoted a separate book to titled: ***'Get programmed to be the greatest one-day batsman in the world'***.

There are a lot of holes and blanks and ambiguities which lie inbetween being given a bat and being simply told to get a century and actually knowing what it will take and what you have to do to get a century, and this book seeks to fill in these blanks and holes and teach you on a fine level of granularity exactly how you must bat and what you must do with it in order to actually perform, succeed and get a century. That is, we hand hold you through each mental thought process and bodily movement required in batting in a step by step and linear fashion so there are no ifs and buts as to what you have to do to actually perform your duty as a batsman.

By reading these linear instructions and being shown in a step by step manner exactly how to choose your stroke and how to strike at the ball, you are efectually being given the cure to cancer and the whole act of batting mapped out for you to own in your custody and refer to as a definitive and conclusive reference which can be relied upon to determine stroke selection to any possible scenario which exists.

Diagram 19: depiction of z-box when not in form **OR** ball swinging too much

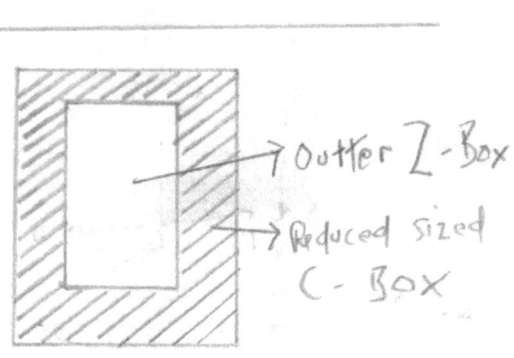

So we see from the diagram the z-box or the good accurate ball zone gets bigger and the concentration box gets smaller. This in effect means we are struggling to see the ball or the ball is swinging around too much or we are having difficulty getting on top of the pitch and bowling. This effectively implicates that we are striking at less deliveries and our scoring options or c-box have now been reduced or shrunken.

So this is what we call the 4 layers of visual acuity which all great batsman base their visualization and stroke selection process around. Either the z-box gets smaller and c-box gets bigger and we are attacking and pouncing on a wider range of deliveries regards line and length; or the z-box gets bigger and the c-box gets smaller and we are playing defense to a larger array of deliveries regarding line and length.[3]

Anything outside of the c-box can be played without any degree of close attention or attentiveness as it is too far wide, full or short and you can just playing without even having to think, as is said.

So now you know there is a certain visualization protocol implicated in cricket and there are certain circumstances under which we change our z –box to be bigger or smaller. You also understand that there is a plethora almost a smorgasbord of stroke making opportunities whilst and wherein the ball lands in the loose c-box range, and that the batsman is under extreme pressure to concentrate and calculate what the optimal shot is and exactly which stroke he is going to offer.

---

[3] For a full treatment on the c-box read our book specialised on stroke selection and how exactly to see, judge, pick and play deliveries landing within the c-box.

Chapter 6
PLAYING THE ERRATICALLY SWINGING BALL:

So what do we do when the ball is swinging around and swinging around big? Well the first thing we do is increase the size of our z-box to an outer z-box, and the second thing we do is not to try to strike the ball too hard but only rely on caressing the ball with timing and let the ball come to you and greet it with soft hands. When the ball is swinging erratically there is the biggest chance of an outside edge occurring and getting caught behind; **AND** the chance of the ball sneaking through the bat and pad for a bowled or an LBW. How do we counteract this? Well, all we can do is play late and with soft hands and keep our focus of vision or gaze on the outer z-box. The bowler has now forced you into a state of submission and you must have you own clever tactics to counteract this. You must play defense and play with soft hands and let the ball come to you and merely rely on caressing and stroking the ball as opposed to attacking the ball, and you must aim to pick up singles and 1s and 2s and 3s . All's you can do is play with utmost caution, vigilance and attentiveness and wait for the loose ball for a boundary hitting stroke.

Bowlers who get erratic swing are the biggest threat in cricket and to some extent the batsman really is forced into submission and made to be a sitting duck. **DO NOT** get too impetuous and just protect your wicket with sound defensive technique, and remember to go forward and not back to the ball in that forwardish accurate ball zone to protect yourself from the in-swinger. Also learn to drop the hands and let the ball go outside off stump if the bowler is getting substantial outwards way movement on the offside so that you can protect yourself from the caught behind in slips.

Play and pick the line *'sequentially'* and not in *'parallel'*. This basically means to watch and wait a bit longer as the ball journeys down the pitch and get a better look at the line until a later but not too later moment, before you commit to your stroke[4].

When the bowler is consistently getting swing and lateral ways movement in both directions, it is imperative that you play the ball late and with soft hands and simply try to maneuver the ball around for 1s and 2s. Also make sure you keep the pad and bat close together. Playing the erratically swinging delivery is not easy but there are ways and means and techniques we can use to not be bullied by the pace and swing the bowler is getting. The main technique is to use the sequential method by which to pick the line of any given delivery. There is a thing called the z-box and the L-point in batting, which is most critical whilst playing the erratically swinging ball or any ball for that matter. Inspect our diagram below:

Diagram 20: picking line by L-point

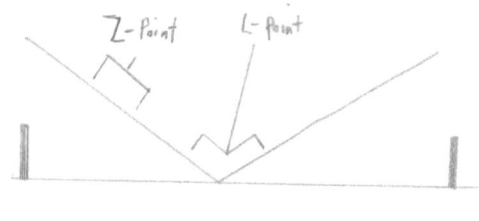

---

[4] We have talked about the 2 methods of picking line in our other book titled: 'get programmed to become the best one-day batsman ever' – make sure you read it!

So the z- point is the time by which we pick the length of the ball, which as we discussed, is centred around deducing the behavior of the ball. The **'L-point'** comes slightly after the **'z-point'** and allows us to get a better look at the swing and seam off the pitch a little better and is the point by which you should have picked the line. You have now picked length **AND** line and are ready to make a decisive foot movement and choose your stroke.

So just remember, don't feel defeated if the bowler has forced you into a state of submission via the erratically swinging delivery. There are means and ways for you to survive this onslaught and barrage of accurate swinging deliveries the bowler is subjecting you to. Just be patient and remain composed and wait for the loose delivery and until the just keep relying on merely maneuvering the ball around via soft hands and playing the ball late.

The biggest thing when the ball is swinging erratically is that you need to get a clear picture of the line late but not too late and and you must to some extent sacrifice the big scoring and boundary hitting strokes – this is the only way to handle the erratically swinging delivery.

Chapter 7
BATTING WHEN THERE IS NO DEVIATION:

Batting when the bowler is consistently **NOT** getting any lateral ways movement is a batsman's dream. For when this happens an elite batter is so well trained and honed that he can virtually treat any and every ball, bar the Yorker, as a scoring opportunity and there is no such thing as a good line or a good length **OR** even both.

The whole idea and crux upon which elite batting is based around is when the bowler is getting movement and the batsman really must concentrate hard and watch the ball hard and sacrifice certain strokes from his artillery of strokes he has up his sleeve – usually 3-5. But when the ball is not deviating there is a plethora of unorthodox and improvised shots that batsmen can play.

When there is no deviation there is no such thing as a z-box and an outer one or an inner one, and if skilled enough, a batsman can really crack his whip and leave the bowler and bowling in shambles. It is deviation and the playing of the deviating ball is what constitutes the whole chore and mission of playing cricket and batting in elite level cricket – both for batter and bowler alike.

If the bowler did not have any varieties and generate movement in the air and off the pitch, then at a higher level of cricket would essentially be rendered useless as the batsmen are so well trained, honed and sharpened that without a deviating delivery he can play all sorts of ingenious and risky shots which can really put the bowler with his wall to the back. Just as in street cricket where the ball doesn't swing and the batsman is in control, in charge and has the advantage; a similar thing happens in representative cricket wher the bowler does not generate swing – he can treat you as simply just some random bowler from the street and make you look silly. Without getting deviation and swing and lateral ways movement, it is like a high quality seasoned champion of world cricket like Tendulkar facing up to some random playing street cricket and not getting the ball to deviate. And we all know who is going to be the victor here!

Our last words are to not abuse the advantage this game of cricket has given you as a batsman and that if the ball is not deviating, really try to cash in on and capitalize with big boundary hitting shots and endeavor to score off of every ball and at a high strike rate.

Chapter 8
Finding the gaps in the field:

It is a batsman's duty and job to score runs and play a good forceful brand of cricket and achieve the end result of actually getting runs any way possible and by any means possible. Orthodox cricket and classical batting technique is all well and fine but the ultimate task of the batsman is to find the gaps anyhow and anyway, even if it involves a degree of risk, improvisation and perilousness.

We can either play the ball on merit and simply play the right shot to the right ball as is said, or we can improvise a little and use various elements of great batting technique to find the gap no matter what the bowler is doing and where he is pitching. Basically, even in orthodox cricket there is usually 2-4 strokes which we can play to any particular ball, however if you are aiming to play for the country you must go beyond the orthodox and percentage style of cricket and have a range of between 3 and 5 shots which you can potentially offer to any particular delivery.

We must focus on timing the ball and piercing the field also and not just focus on hitting each ball for a boundary. Not every ball a bowler is going to bowl will be safely and securely despatchable to the boundary and we must become adept at and perfect our ability to keep the scoring and the runs going by finding the gaps. There is no use in hitting and timing the ball well and playing your shot copy book style if you are not going to find the gap and get runs from it, is there? We must extend and outstretch our ability of merely playing orthodox cricket and playing the right shot to the right ball, if we are to be in contention for playing for the country. We must meticulously hone our ability to play 3-5 shots to the same ball via our net sessions such that come big match day you can simply execute the right shot, out of an array of different shots, and play the shot which can find the gap in the field which lies before you at that moment in time.

Like we said there is orthodox cricket and un-orthodox cricket and it is the un-orthodox cricket which is going to make you a master at finding the gaps. You must be able to hit inside out, outside in, loft the ball over the infield, use deft touch to deflect the ball behind slips and most of all be able to clear the boundary with a six hitting stroke.

Sometimes the opposition captain deliberately puts a gap in the field to lure you and entice you to play a certain risk taking shot and take your wicket that way. This is also something which must be considered whilst batting and conducting your task of finding the gap and is what you could call another parameter in you coming out on top and finding the gap without getting out.

The techniques elite batsman use to find the gap are:

- Opening the face of the bat
- Closing the face of the bat
- Giving the bowler the charge
- Lofting the ball over the infield
- Using the wrists to maneuver the ball into the gap
- Playing inside-out shots
- Playing outside-in shots
- Getting into a pre-meditated position such that you can hit the ball into the gap.
- Deflecting the ball behind slips

Sometimes we see a gap in the field and aim to hit through that gap regardless of where the ball pitches. This involves an element of risk **AND** luck. We say luck because the ball must be pitched in a certain rea and there and there abouts to actually execute your gap finding stroke; and risk because you are doing something unorthodox and may get an edge or a bowled or get out if the ball does not land in roughly the position required to hit the ball through the gap. For example if you are trying to find a gap on the off-side and the bowler pitches on middle or middle and leg stump then suddenly you are taking a risk to hit the ball through the off side as you must get inside the line of the ball and play a stroke which is very unnatural on the body and considered a difficult stroke to play.

When a batsman is aiming for a gap without waiting to see where the ball pitches and not playing an orthodox and *'correct'* shot according to the line and length of the ball, we call this *'pre-meditating your shot'*.

Elite batsman can pre meditate their stroke and aim for a gap and actually succeed in finding it in almost 60% of cases, and successfully executing a pre-meditated shot is something the greatest batsman possess and are capable of doing. If you are looking to play for the country then this particular skill should be improved and competencies in which must be attained.

Chapter 9
Hitting across the line:

Hitting across the line is when we don't present a full face of the bat and play straight, but rather, try to hit through the onside from square leg to mid-wicket as well as hit through the offside between point and cover with an inside out shot. Hitting across the line through the onside is substantially harder than going through the off side but is still a perfectly viable option if the gap **DOES** seem to exist in the off side. There are two methods of hitting across the line. One where we use the bat to come from behind 3rd slip and follow through almost perpendicularly to the line of the ball and then there is the Tendulkar method or the gold standard method where we bring the bat down straight and follow through relatively straight and use the flick of the wrists at last moment to send the ball flying toward where the gap is. The fact is that most occasions where you are required to or have an opportunity to hit across the line is when the ball is directed at the stumps. This is why we use the Tendulkar method. Inspect the following diagrams:

Diagram 21: Hitting across the line without the wrists

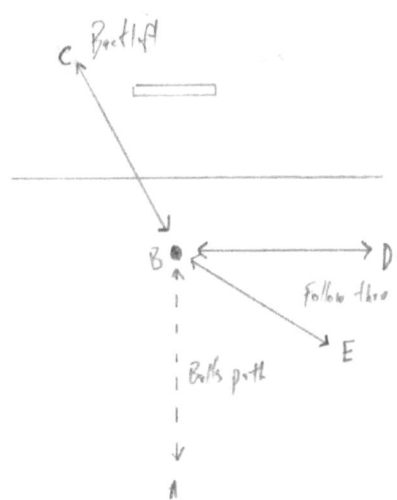

In this method, which is considered the usual method, we hit almost perpendicularly to the line of the ball, that is we follow through with bat face directed at point **D** or **E**. This method is dangerous as if you miss then you are 99% going to get the LBW. That is why the Tendulkar method is a much better option to deploy when required to hit across the line. Inspect the following diagram:

Diagram 22: hitting across the line via use of wrists

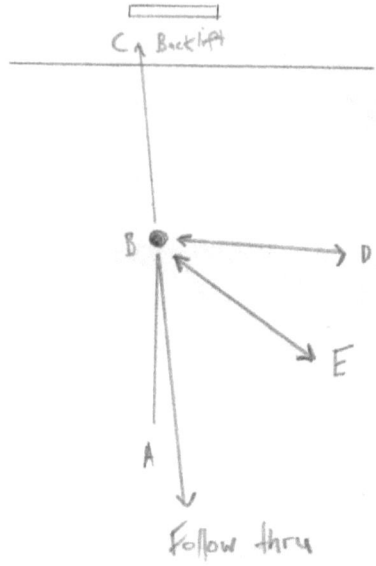

In this method we don't follow through at point **D** or **E** as was in the previous diagram, but rather, we follow through relatively straight, show the full face of the bat leading up to the ball-bat contact and at the last moment give a flick of the wrists.[5] This is what is called the *'Tendulkar method'* or the *'Tendulkar magic'*. This is how Tendulkar minimizes the chances of getting a bowled or LBW when we hit across the line and don't play straight and present the full face of the bat. By using this method of hitting across the line, Tendulkar was able to successfully find gaps with

---

[5] We have not shown you to hit across the line through off-side as this usually involves both directing the bat toward your aim AND using the wrists slightly as well as opening the face of the bat.

ease whilst keeping his wicket, and gathered many runs from hitting across the line without any risk.

Chapter 10
Lofting the Ball Over the Infield:

Sometimes we are required to loft the ball over the infield and sufficiently enough to go over the fielder's head but not necessarily go for six. To hit for six requires power and leverage which is only generated when the arms are free and there is a full flowing motion with the arms, however, to simply clear the infield you need not need more than just a flick of the wrists.

So there are two types or styles to going the aerial route. One being simply jabbing and flicking the ball over any fielders up close or in the mid field and the other winding up and striking the ball with the full force of the arm swing and sometimes hip rotation and hitting for six.

Going the aerial route is something considered an integral skill for the elite batsman to have as it yields 6s and also the 1s and 2s when the ball is lofted over the close in fielder, and is one skill which you should aim to practice if you are serious about playing for the country.

Generally, we can loft the ball and go the aerial route when the ball is either slightly short of a length or slightly forward of a length, as it becomes difficult to loft the ball when it is on a length. The general and common advice is that if pitched on a length **DO NOT** try to open or close the face of the bat, **DO NOT** try to go inside out or vice versa and **DO NOT** try to loft the ball for 6. However, these are just guidelines and you may have the talent to do so but it is generally not recommended as it increases the chances of getting out by ten-fold.

CHAPTER 11
BUILDING AN INNINGS BY PLAYING DEFENSE AT THE START:

Innings building skills is a big part of batting and the consequences of not attaining them can be absolutely dire for the aspiring batsman. Even if you have the talent to score a triple century, if you did not invest in a little sighter period, during which one is to gauge the pitch and bowling and protect himself from the wicket taking ball, then your talent is rendered useless and you have not done justice to your true ability or skill level.

At the start you must get a sighter and gather certain information and data before you can start playing the authoritative brand of batting you are dreaming of playing. This data refers to the bounce or lack thereof in the pitch, the direction the bowler is swinging the ball and by how much, exactly how fast or slow he is, what angle is he coming in to bowl from and last but not least how accurate he is and how consistently he can be accurate for. Upon gathering this information and conducting your sighter period you have successfully acquired the parametrics and factors you need in order to launch an assault or play a more dictating brand of batting.

At the start the threat of the accurate swinging ball is at its peak so we must have something to counteract this! What we do is basically start our innings by playing only in the 'V' and don't play any balls which are away from our body and stumps. Also adjust the back lift to come from dead straight and follow through dead straight, and that too with soft hands. This is such that you don't get an edge and even if you do it will not carry through to the keeper. You must get a sighter the scientific way. You must merely play defense for 3-5 balls and get a sighter in the most scientific manner possible.[6]

We must keep our primary vision open and alert for the good accurate ball which lands with the z-box and only the peripheral vision open to punishing the loose delivery, we must straighten our back lift and follow through straight showing the full face of the bat, we must **NOT** hit across the line unless the ball sufficiently short or full enough, and we must basically play to our L-box, which we diagrammatically depicted before. We will depict it again. This essentially implicates that we only keep focused and hyper alert to the z-box and only dare to play an attacking shot when the ball lands in that bad line **AND** length zone. Inspect the following diagram:

---

[6] The exact and intricate science behind getting a sighter is discussed at length in our book titled: 'Get programmed to be the greatest one-day batsman ever'.

Diagram: 23: building an innings by only striking at balls which are of a bad line **AND** length:

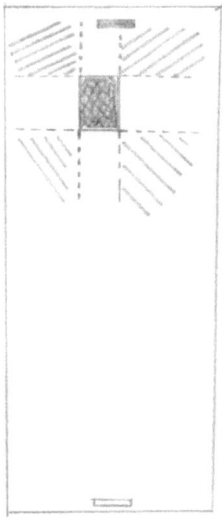

We then gradually advance to hitting and striking any ball which lands outside of the z-box – once we have gotten a sighter that is![7] We **MUST** be patient and deploy a scientific and methodical approach whilst getting ourselves a sighter, or else we will give our wicket away cheaply and be back in the pavilion before we had a chance for our stroke making abilities to actually flourish and blossom.

If you are to keep your wicket and allow the fun part to actually start, which is ideally playing to a reduced sized z-box and an increased sized c-box and be in complete command and control,

---

[7] This is explained and shown in depth in the book about Sehwag and one-day batting

you **MUST** adjust your visionary process **AND** chose which balls to attempt a scoring nshot off and which not! You must note that even when we are getting a sighter and are cutting out many of the shots possible in batting, we **ARE** allowed to pull the short ball and drive at the pitched up one.[8]

So play in the 'V' and only focus your gaze on the z-box, which represents the good line **AND** length ball and gather some key data about the pitch and bowling before you try to unleash the full repertoire of strokes you may have up your sleeve. Abstain and restrain yourself and discipline yourself to refrain from not playing an attacking shot unless it lies within any one of the 4 L-boxes. Batting is all about making your own lady luck and not leaving anything to chance – this is why we must get our sighter the diligent and conscientious way.

---

[8] In regards to the pitched up one, be weary if the bowler is generating tremendous amounts of swing and/or late swing before you attempt to drive during the sighter period!

CHAPTER 12
ESTIMATING AND DETERMINING THE Z-BOX ASAP:

Where the z-box will lie depends on a few parametrics which we must account for before we can confidently say this is where the z-box is for any given pitch and any given bowler. It is quite simple! There are two factors which determine where your z-box or good line and length ball will lie at. The key reason we need to determine our z-box is so we can know for sure what is at a driving length and what is not and what is a short ball and what is not. These 2 key factors or parametrics are the height of the bowler and the bounciness or lack-thereof in the pitch, both of which decide what is an accurate ball and what is not. Inspect the following diagrams which reveal how the z-box moves according to the metrics we just mentioned

Diagram 24: pitch is keeping low

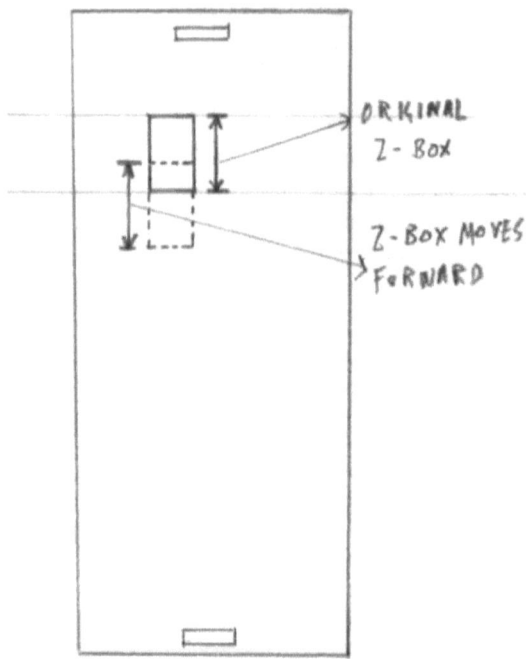

Diagram 25: pitch is bouncy

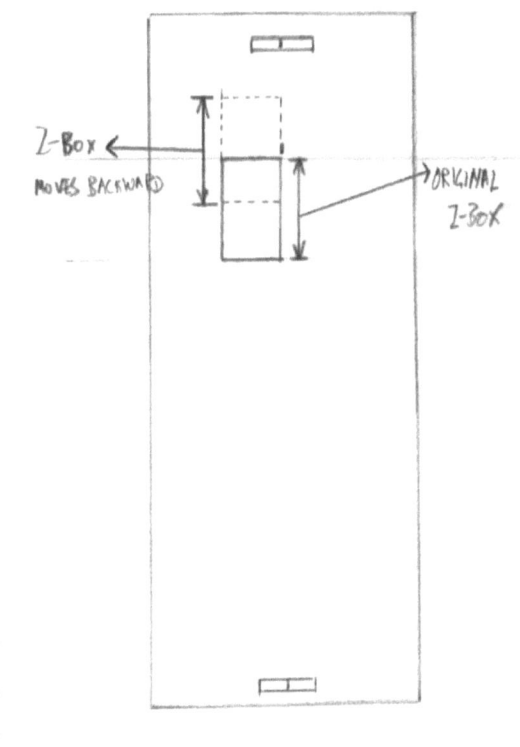

This may seem like a difficult concept and diagram or idea to understand but **ABSOLUTELY MUST** be engrained if you are to have the confidence to play on different pitches and know what is a good length and what is not and most importantly what is at a driving length and what is at a pulling length and what is not.

In so far as the height of the bowler, which we revealed as the second parametric in deciding where the good length ball zone lies and what is full enough to drive and what is short enough to pull, inspect the following diagrams:

Diagram 26: bowler is taller

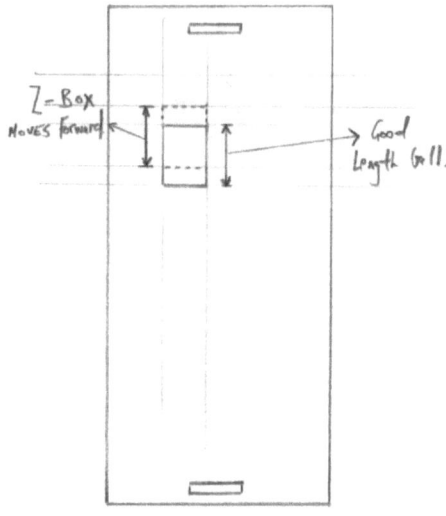

So the taller the bowler the z-box moves forward or towards the stumps. What was before a full delivery anding outside of z-box is now a good accurate ball and the one that was in a good length zone is now short and can be pulled or cut with ease.

Our job as batsman is to score runs and score them in the fastest and swift manner possible. We are not there to merely show our faces on the field and keep watching and observing the ball but to actually strike at the ball. In order to fulfill our roles as specialist batsmen, we must get through our little sighter period as quickly as possible and size up the pitch and bowling in the most brisk and expeditious manner possible. You must wait, be patient and play defense for 4 – 7 balls in order to get a feel for the bowling and pitch and really define your z-box to the most minute precision, if you are to go on and dominate the bowling and get a big score. When the bowler is shorter the following happens:

Diagram 27: bowler is shorter

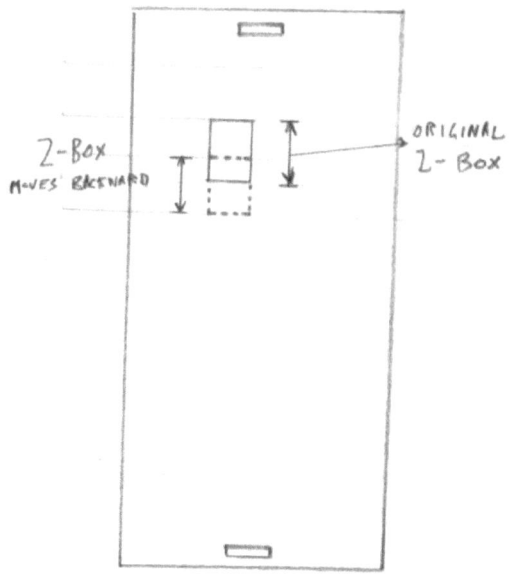

So for the shorter bowler the good length accurate ball moves forward and what was at a short enough length to cut and pull is now part of that good length accurate ball zone. The one which was in good accurate ball zone is now full of a length and can be dealt with via the straight drive, on-drive or cover-drive.

We must determine this to the precision of say 1.5 to 2 cricket balls width or diameter if we are to play any type of a forceful and attacking brand of batting, and once again may not make sense immediately but is **THE ONE SKILL** you **ABSOLUTELY MUST** know if you are a batsman, so study it, look over it and mull over it in your mind a little and understand the logic behind how and why the z-box moves. You will NOT have what it takes to survive your sighter period without understanding this and will just never have the confidence about what a loose delivery is and what is **NOT** without grasping this phenomenon of why and how the *'z-box'* shifts forward or back according to the height and bounce in the pitch

"UNDERSTAND THIS LITTLE PIECE OF SCIENCE AND YOU WILL FEEL LIKE A KING ON HIS THROWN AGAINST ANY BOWLING AND ANY PITCH".

The more accurately and quickly you can size up the pitch and bowling the more chances you have of dominating the bowling and playing a long innings and it is this very skill which lets most talented batsmen down – the ability to get a sighter and size up the pitch and bowling sooner rather than later. Getting played in quickly and not wasting too much time on gathering the data about the bowler and the pitch is the 1st thing you must do if you are to start choosing your stroke with precision and exactness.

CHAPTER 13
MAXIMISING SCORING POTENTIAL FROM WITHIN THE C-BOX:

As you now know about this thing called the c-box and what it represents and how it gets bigger or smaller depending on the exact z-box you are adhering by: either middle, inner or outer; we can now get cracking and show you what you need to know on a mental platform exactly what it is and what it's implications are to you as a serious batsman in both test and one-day cricket.

Most batsman have 1 maybe 2 or at the most 3 shots which they can feasibly offer to any given delivery – deliveries which land within the c-box that is. But if we aspiring to be great and play for the country then you must have 3-5! Let us use a diagram to show you how the c-box works or should work. Inspect the below diagram.

Diagram 28: The elite batsman's treatment of the c-box

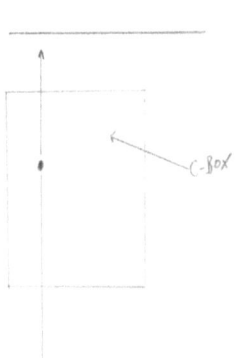

So we see the ball lands within c-box – that is obvious. We see that it lands outside off stump and just a little short of a length.

What do we do? What would an elite and seasoned batsman do? Well, there are 3-5 shots which one should have up your sleeve and you will decide which one you will play based on where the gap in the field is and based on which shot will yield more runs.

You can play the square cut shot easily, you can play the late cut easily, you can play the pull shot easily and you can play the flick through mid-wicket not easily but you can still play it if required. You can also play the swat off front foot straight back down the ground with a flat bat and you can also play the drive on the rise or on the up also not easily but you still **CAN** play it if required. So there are about 4-6 shots which you have up your sleeve and should be prepared and ready to play – it just depends on where the gap in the field is on the day. Likewise, for any other line and length there is also an array or subset of strokes which **CAN** and **SHOULD** be played[9].

It is your skill and versatility in regards playing the c-box and having 4-6 shots up your sleeve which can possibly be brought to the table according to where the gap is, is what it will take for you to play for the country. At the national level batsman are expected the get the runs any how and any way and **MUST** and **SHOULD** have what it takes to respond to anything within the *'c-box'* with maximum due diligence, precision and stealth, such that the maximum yield is generated in the form of runs scored.

---

[9] This is thoroughly explained and illustrated within the other book *'Get programmed to be the greatest one-day batsman ever'*

Chapter 14
BATTING TECHNIQUE:

Batting technique refers to the bodily movement and physical movement in the form of the hands, wrists, elbows and feet required whilst conducting sound, stable and quality batting. Also using the top hand in combination with the bottom hand. In this chapter we are going to show you what to do with all the body parts aforementioned.

Use the elbow as a power generator and field placer, use the wrists to flick the ball through the onside, use soft hands to deaden the impact of ball on bat such that you don't get a caught behind, use the bottom hand to play powerful cuts and pulls, use the elbow in combination with the top hand to play your defensive shot.

This game cricket is not all about cover drives all along the ground and fine leg glances but is embodied by the techniques and methods of professional base-ballers also. All the horizontal bat shots and anything requiring a strong bottom-hand dominance essentially equates to the fact that a batsman in cricket is to some extent playing the role of and emulating the technique used in baseball per say. We can use the strong bottom hand dominance to play the swat shot straight back past the bowler and of course the cut shot for 6 and the pull shot for 6. So batting also resembles baseball to some extent and the strong bottom handed dominance shots are just as important in cricket as they are in baseball and in fact fetch more runs! Use the feet to get yourself and your body in to position and perfectly place yourself to play the shot correctly and competently.

One must adjust his technique whilst playing the different formats of the game, but further, during certain stages and situation the game is in. For example the opening batsman facing up to the new hard ball, or batting towards the death overs or whether it is test cricket or one-day cricket.

When fresh to the crease you must aim to have a less cocked back lift and play straight and present the full face of the bat as well as play with soft hands and let the ball come to you. It is the 1st 15 balls of a batsman's innings which makes or breaks his hopes of getting a big score at a decent run rate and these technical adjustments are **ABSOLUTELY** necessary for the elite batter playing against elite bowlers, if they are to go on and make a decent score.

Knowing what guard to take is also somewhat of a scientific task. Whether it is middle, middle and leg or leg? How do we know? Well usually and typically we take middle stump guard but there are scenarios and circumstances in which we **MUST** alter our guard. For example, if the bowler is left arm over the wicket and getting the ball to swing in to the pads and at brisk pace, then we **MUST** take a middle and leg or leg stump guard. Or if you are a masterful player through the offside, like Ganguly or Ranatunga, then again we take a leg stump guard to give ourselves room to glide the ball through the offside even if it is pitched on leg stump or middle stump. Seldom if ever to we take the middle and off or off stump guard – it is usually a decision between middle, middle and leg **OR** leg in regards which guard a batter takes. Depending on the line the bowler is bowling and if he IS bowling around off stump or marginally outside **AND** you want to hit through onside, then we can adopt the middle and off **OR** off stump guard to give ourselves the chance to get outside the line of the ball and flick through midwicket or square-leg areas.

Technique must be adjusted according to the age of the ball also. Whether the ball is new and hard or whether it is old and softer – these variables must be accounted for and our technique adjusted accordingly. When the ball is new and hard we merely have to time the ball and it will go for 4; when the ball is new it might reflect off the pitch at a greater pace than you may have anticipated, when the ball is new it may swing a little more. These are all variables which warrant an adjustment in our technique and mental process and can mean the difference between getting out cheaply or making a hundred.

The softer ball is usually easier to play then the newer ball and it is for that reason you usually see your best most talented batsmen come in at 4th drop. When the ball is new it is hard and reflects off the bat at a greater speed and it is for this reason that our most courageous and technically solid batsmen are sent in to open the innings. This is merely a matter of cricketing logic, principle and theory and it does not mean that the middle order can't generate greater bat speed when the ball is old or the batsman must be perfectly technically sound in order to open the innings. These are just theories which apply in most cases but maybe not all!

When the ball is new and hard you get full value for your horizontal bat shots and can drive the ball for 4 merely with touch and timing; whereas when the ball is old, yes, it doesn't swing as much and is easier played in that regard, but it is harder to play as you have to force and generate the force and motion to actually hit the ball long and hard.

One of the most potent and tacit skills for a batsman to have is playing the ball on the rise or on the up. This is usually practiced and developed on cement pitches which are perfectly true but is a shot which all the great batsman who play on turf also possess in their kit of armory. To play on the rise the ball must be just short of a length and sufficiently short to get underneath it but at the same time sufficiently full in order to play the ball under your eyes and be able to get on top of it to some extent. Aravinda De Slva of Sri Lanka was perhaps the perfect exponent of someone who could prey on anything marginally short to play on the up. There were many but this is a very power oriented stroke and requires you to get on top of the ball with a maximally high elbow and hit through the ball with a fully cocked back lift.

Test match and one-day formats of the game are like completely different ball games and require certain technical adjustments to be made for one to cope up with and revel under the pressure which is abound at the highest level of cricket. Generally, in test matches we take a longer time to get a sighter, play with a lower cocked back lift, make the bowler bowl to you and not offer a shot to the swinging ball on the off stump, try not to hit across the line so much and basically play to a larger sized z-box and take your time to get a feel for the pitch and bowling before you start playing an attacking brand of cricket or batsmanship.

In one day cricket there is less time to get a sighter and the batsman must to some extent be able to hit the ground running and not need the sighter period. Generally play with a fully cocked and high back lift position and only lower the backlift and play in the 'V' for 5-10 balls. Aim to generate maximum bat speed via bringing your back lift around to 3rd slip and don't be afraid to hit across the line.

If you are to play for the country then you must be able to adapt or switch between the different formats of the game and switch into test mode or one-day mode smoothly and without any hiccups or aberrations. We have defined the major differences in the two formats and given you an idea as to how to adjust your technique correspondingly, and you now should have no problem as far as what you have to do differently and how you are to do it.[10]

Another explicative skill for a batsman to have is playing the short ball off of front foot. This is one shot only Tendulkar and a handful of others had the capacity to play and is considered a revered talent in the game of cricket, especially in modern times. To do this one must basically swat or slap the ball with the bottom hand and put tremendous amounts of bat speed into the shot.

Use of the feet is a very important and critical facet to batting technique which simply cannot be ignored whilst training and practicing to be elite cricketers. You must know how and when to use the feet to dance down the track and play a lofted shot and where exactly you have to plant your feet for any given line. Yes, depending on the line we make our foot movements to be either straight down the pitch or more move your feet through the onside and hit the ball through the off side. This has all been explained in our book titled *'Sculpting you to be the next master batsman: Sachin Tendulkar'.* Generally we use the charge tactic to smother the spin if it is a spin bowler **OR** get underneath the ball if it is a pacer such that we can loft the ball for 6.

Yet another aspect to technique whilst playing the higher levels is the ability to play the full ball off back foot and play the short ball off front foot. This is an advanced skill which only some batsmen

---

[10] The exact how to do it is what is explicitly and elaborately shown and discussed within the specialised coaching manuals on batting. Please read them for the full run down.

have but if you are aiming to play for the country, then is something you must practice, hone and train for.

If one is to play for the country then he must have all the shots in the book and more. Here is a list of the typical cricketing shots which we often speak of in cricket and in batting:

- On-drive
- Off-drive
- Straight-drive
- Cover-drive
- Square-cut
- Late-cut
- Leg glance
- Pull-shot
- Hook-shot
- Square-drive
- Drive through mid-wicket
- Flick off the pads
- Cow-shot
- Drive on the rise
- Back foot punch

There are obviously more shots including lofted and inside out and flick shots, but almost all shots in batting are a derivative or a combination of the above-mentioned typical or standard ones.

The hallmarks and cornerstones of sound, stable and orthodox batting technique which you will need to remember whilst practicing and playing cricket are:

- Elbow up
- Head down
- Bat-speed whilst playing attacking shots
- Straight bat in defence
- Foot to the pitch of the ball
- Bat and pad close together
- Good temperament
- Shot-selection
- Playing in the-V
- Eye on the ball
- Good timing
- Use of the wrists in 'flicking' the ball to onside
- Playing through the ball with the hands
- Use of soft hands whilst defending and playing late cuts
- Picking the length and seeing the ball well – having a good eye
- Playing on both sides of the wicket
- Let the ball come to you

- Make the bowler bowl to you[11]
- Building an innings through patience, shot-selection, concentration and a sound defensive technique

Along with keeping our eye on the ball, keeping our head down and accounting for the length ball early in our innings by playing with a dead straight bat, these are just some of the things which come to mind when we think of good batting and correct batting technique and a brand of batting which is necessary to reach the national levels..

---

[11] Play ball close to the body only and don't flirt or chase the ball outside off stump

CHAPTER 15
CHOOSING YOUR STROKE:

Within the realms of orthodox cricket per say there is only one and only one shot to play to any given ball, but this is not the mindset of the cricketer of the modern era. Today's batsmen have to have 3-5 shots up their sleeves and be able to pick the right one according to the situations at the time and at that moment. With the advent and popularization and commercialization of the IPL, the whole task of choosing your stroke has suddenly become a very hyper-critical and finicky task which must be done to the utmost of precision and exactness. That is, the batsmen of today's era are under all the more pressure to play the exact and correct stroke to any given ball than ever before and suddenly the act of choosing your stroke in a game of cricket has become a multi-billion dollar business. For the full description about choosing your shot and dealing with your c-box in the most optimal and advantageous manner, read our other book titled: *'Get programmed to be the greatest oneday batsman ever'.*

Stroke selection and choosing the right stroke comes down to a thing called conditional logic which we have discussed at length in our father book as well as our book about Sehwag, and need not be explicitly discussed in this book. For now just take on board that choosing your stroke among possibilities is not only a highly critical part of batting but something which is treated within a factual context as a vast subject domain in that there is so much to learn and understand about what shots to play to what balls and having the ability to play 4-6 shots to any given ball – hence why we have devoted a whole book to it (get programmed to be the greatest one-day batsman ever). Vector reading and prudent shot selection is **ALL BATTING IS ABOUT**, and we urge you to read the book about Sehwag for a complete and through grasp on the subject and a book which has been dubbed the most scientific and explicit book written on cricket in the last 100 years.

As you will come to know there is a certain science known as conditional logic which must be brought to the table for one to perfect and choose their stroke among possibilities, and that this is the very crux and bare bones and skeleton of what batting is about.

"Cricket is just a game centered around reading vector forces and prudent stroke selection – nothing more"

……………Nikhil

The biggest lesson you must learn regards choosing your stroke pertains to knowing when to attempt a big scoring and/or risky shot and when not to and choosing your ball to hit. If you can master stroke selection and know which ball should be hit hard and which should not, then you are well on your way to playing first class cricket down the track. Don't be silly and not use conditional logic to guide you and usher you as to what the appropriate stroke or strokes are to any given line and length.

Another parametric which decides how you will choose your stroke is the age of the ball. If the ball is hard and shiny and/or swinging then treat the z-box with utmost of importance and criticality and don't hit across the line to anything within a good length zone as the ball is swinging and the possibility of getting the edge is at its peak.

Choose your ball to hit and once you have made up your mind follow through with your decision with your whole heart and might and do not be half-hearted. The trick is to know which ball to choose as your big scoring shot and which ball to treat with more circumspection. There is a simple formula or rule in cricket as strike hard if the ball is **TOO** short, full or wide; but the reality is that there is a plethora of possible strokes which can yield runs apart from the deliveries which are merely too short, far and wide, but also ones which are only semi loose or semi-bad deliveries. These balls also require punishment and if you are to play for the country you must be able to *'take a yard if given an inch'*.

Stroke selection is a large topic domain as there are literally dozens of ways in which to hit the same ball and several inputs, variables or determinants in deciding which stroke to play to which ball. We will not go into them in depth as they have been explained by some 300 lines of linear computer programming code within our book about sehwag and perfect one-day batting.

Just remember for now to choose your ball judiciously when you want to hit hard and long and execute the stroke whole-heartedly and with all your might as well as hone your powers of taking a yard if given just an inch and really try to be in control and have 3-5 strokes which you can unveil to any delivery. Also develop the tenacity to prey on anything only marginally loose in regards line and/or length.

Remember, you are a chooser and not a beggar and have 3-5 possible shots you can play to any given delivery. The only challenge remaining now is to play the right one according to where the gap in the field is.

Just remember this is a somewhat advanced skill in cricket, playing 3-5 shots to the any given delivery that is, and may take a bit of practice in the nets. It is highly recommended you read our book: ***'Get programmed to be the greatest oneday batsman ever'***, if you are serious about being a chooser and not a beggar and having 3-5 shots up your sleave to any given delivery and go on to become a master onedat batsman.

Chapter 16
Handling pressure:

When you are playing serious cricket and not just a past time but to either get selected for the state or country or even perform for the state or the country then you will always inadvertently face extreme pressures to perform. The stakes are high through one form or the other and the jaws of defeat must be avoided at any cost, such that you can make a sturdy contribution to the team winning. Having said this most seasoned and serious cricketers know how to stay calm under pressure and appreciate the fact that one can only try his best and do whatever is humanly possible to the most faultless standard.

Cricket is a highly pressure packed sport as there are so many things which can go wrong and so many things you must ensure are going right, in order to effectually put up a good show and brand of cricket. To succeed at the top level and play for the country you must have what it takes to come out on top under pressure and counteract the opposition's clever plans. It is this methodical and impregnable quality which can make or break your hopes of playing at the rep level and is something more to do with the mind as opposed bodily movement and technique. You must know what exactly is demanded of you at that point in time and how you are going to do it if you are to survive the pressures of higher level cricket and you must know what exactly is the calculation and requirement for victory without being explicitly told. You should have on an individual basis a good track of the game and it's situation and what is required of you to effectively guide the team closer and closer to victory, if you are to be considered a mature and valuable addition to the team or squad of the national team.

It is when one knows exactly what is required of him and exactly how he is going to endeavour to achieve it that the ability to handle pressure ultimately stems from. We see the greatest technician and shrewdest cricketing mind ever to play the game Sachin tendulkar, never feel overwhelmed by the pressure of the situation irrespective of how n=big or the enormity of the situation seems.

If you are to go one and play national levels then pressure is going to surround you like a pack of wolves hungry for their prey and the only way you are going to overcome and outclass this pressure is via a thorough and apt understanding of the hidden science behind the game – both batting and bowling.

Handling and coming out triumphant in the face of adversity and pressure is a rather intricate subject domain on its own and something which we will discuss in depth within our next book entitled: *'The Psychology and Game theory behind cricket'.*

There are certain finer and intricate responses and/or guards we must bring in to play if a bowler or batter is going to effectively come out on top in the face of pressure and adversity, and we are going to talk about them one by one within our next book, but for now just acknowledge that handling pressure is one of the finer skills and facets to cricket which is also based around a scientific approach and rigour – just like the other aspects of cricket we have talked about. **Science and understanding the science is EVERYTHING in cricket** and you **MUST NOT** miss out on the opportunity to gain an exact understanding of this science which is going to give you the confidence to deal with pressure situations.

CHAPTER 17
THE 2 STAGES OF BATTING DEVELOMENT:

Cricket is the sort of game where everyone wants to be a batsman and the number of budding batsman in the ranks trying to crack the state or national side is insane. There are only 11 spots in the team and not everyone can succesfully forge a career out of cricket and be appreciated for their batting prowesses and abilities. Why is this so? Well it is because there is a distinct difference between a good and a great and there is a distinct difference between a batsman who has the know-how to succeed in firstclass cricket and one who does not. There are millions of batsman out there who look good in the nets, have good technique and are very well adept at hitting through the ball with power and authority, but do they know how to actually score runs under testing conditions and on various pitch surfaces and against the more tactile bolwers and most of all do they know how to actually find the gap on real live match day against a field which is there to make life hard for them?

This is the difference between a good net batsman and a good real life match situation batsman. We see budding batsman in the nets hitting through the ball with power and finesse and ones who can hit the ball far, but remember this is cricket not baseball! We must be able to maneuver into gaps and consistently find the gaps via placing the ball and most importantly we must be able to hit the ball and conduct our innings such that we don't get caught in the outfield.

Most of these fellows we watch in the nets, yes, have achieved a certain amount of skill and mastery over the act of batting, but whence put in a real life match situation you will find that 90% of them will get out caught as they were simply trying to hit the ball hard without thinking about placement and finding the gap which may lie anywhere on real life match day.

This is the difference between a batsman who can go onto play for the country and one who can not. We call this the *'Two stages of batting development'*.

The guys you are seeing in the nets have only achieved mastery over the 1st stage of batting development and not the second and this is why they are not able to put up match performances in real live matches and the reason why they are not able to be picked for the country.

So the 1st stage basically involves seeing the ball well, hitting through the line of the ball for most of your shots, having the ability to play most of the orthodox cricketing shots and being able to bat on synthetic and not turf – which is a different ball game all together. There are millions of such batsman around the world and floating around within the ranks – ones who have not taken their game to the next level and ones who are what you could call only amateur and not professional.

It is the honing in of the skill set demanded to attain mastery over the second stage of batting development is what is the hard part and the part which is going to give you a substantially increased chance of playing for the country. What are these skill sets?

Well sometimes we don't want to wallop the ball and hit through the ball as such but rather use the pace to deflect it into the gap behind the wicket. And usually, we don't want to just blindly hit through the ball and loft it but ensure we are actually going to clear the boundary and hit for 6. And sometimes we don't want to play the orthodox shot to any given delivery, but rather play the one which is going to find the gap.[12] And sometimes we don't want to just drive along the ground but loft the ball over the infield for a 4 or just loft it so far that it goes for 6. And sometimes the shot we are trying to play in order to find the gap may require us to go onto front foot rather than back foot and vice versa.

These are all things which we associate with the second stage of mastery over batting and things which are required of you if aiming to play for the country and not just be a district cricketer or one who only looks good in the nets – we call this the second stage of developing mastery over the act of batting.

It basically comes down to the idea of the c-box we introduced earlier and how best and optimally we are able to negotiate it and play run yielding shots. So it takes a better alertness and awareness as to where in the c-box the ball is landing and what are the stroke making options open to you for that given ball, and playing the right shot and the one which is going to optimise you not getting out and at the same time scoring runs from it relatively risk free.

So power as well as finesse and the ability to play 360 degrees around the wicket with a mature approach to the ball landing within c-box range is what it is going to take for you to raise your game sufficiently enough to say that you have accomplished and achieved the second stage of batting development.

---

[12] This shot does not have to be a shot out of a science fiction novel and can be a completely normal orthodoc cricketing shot. As we said batsman should have 3-5 shots up their sleeve if they are to get runs at that level of cricket!

Whilst training in the nets we often forget about what will be required of us on live match day and fail to practice, train and prepare properly for this very happening. We are not just practicing and playing in the nets for fun but to get a good warm up and practice for showing maturity and the fact that we have accomplished the second stage of batting development come real live match day. Training routine is everything if you want to play for the country and you must take the preparation process for the big game seriously and really hone your powers of playing good cricket and not just good baseball and you must really hone in on your powers of playing 3-5 different shots to the same ball.

Turf cricket, which will be the surface if you are to play national level cricket, demands of you a very rigourous and scientific mindset and approach and a certain visualisation process in order to both protect your wicket **AND** score runs also – as you know from prior chapters in the book.

So practice playing good hard authoritative cricket and hit through the line of the ball but don't forget to practice the second stage of batting development and prime yourself up to hit the ball 360 degreed around the park at will. Alls this will take is the honing in of and proficiency of playing your c-box. Practice playing drives on the rise, late cuts, lofting the ball over the infield, deflecting the ball behind slips and behind the wicket via deft touch and finesse and last but not least try hitting the semi loose ball for 4 or 6.

You may not appreciate this talk of the c-box but once you start practicing hard, get more experienced and start seeing the ball like a football, you realise the subtle differences in where exactly within the c-box the ball lands and the subtle adjustment to your stroke which you are in effect able to do and do so such that you can find the gap in the field.

Chapter 18
THE 2 METHODS OF PICKING LINE:

Picking the line is a lot harder than picking the length as we have no rule such as Euclid's law to guide us, however with a bit of understanding can be done to good effect. We are going to keep it brief so we don't confuse you as what we are about to present to you is a little scientific.

There are 2 methods of picking line – the *'sequential'* method and the *'parrallel'* method. Both rely on something we have called the z-point. One requires of you to estimate, judge and act upon the ball by *'z-point'* and the other requires you watch a little further and setimate, judge and act upon the ball by *'L-point'*. Inspect the following diagram before we go any further:

Diagram 29: 2 methods of picking line

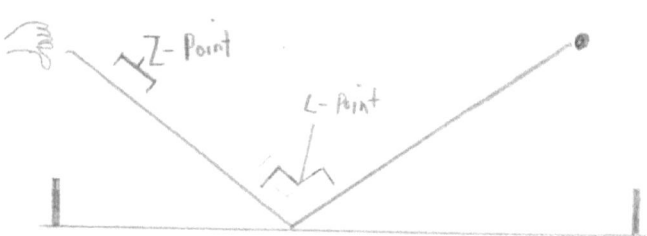

So for the parallel method we pick line and length by the same time – the z-point, and for the sequential method we pick the length by z-point but we wait a little further and pick the line by L-point. Both methods have their advantageds and disadvantages. The idea behind picking the line by L-point as opposed to z-point is so that we can get a better look at the balls shape and how much or wether or not it is swinging or not before we committ to our shot. The advantage of doing this is so that you have a better chance of plying the correct line incase the ball deviates and adopts a different line whilst it is journeying down the picth. The disadvantage is that we can't committ tour stroke early enough to generate batspeed and wind up our bacjlift and hit with more power and authority.

By picking the line in parallel we are able to get a good bat swing and hit through the ball with more conviction and power and hit through the line of the ball. But what happens if it swings? Then you are in trouble. But as long as the ball doesn't swing by too much we shouldn't encounter any problems. Also, we get our bodies in position to play the line **AND** length by z-point and thenif the ball deviates we simply make a late adjustment to the new line via the hands and wrists.

Different situations and conditions call for the deployment of one of either of these two techniques. For example if you are playing test cricket and the ball is deviating then we better off waiting til L-point to judge line and play our stroke late and according to the correct and actual line. Yes, this generally robs us of the batspeed and power we could have generated had we picked line by z-point, but then we can always use the wrists and hands to give a strong flick and still be able to hit powerfully.[13]

Picking the line the parallel method **DOES** come with its risks, but what can you do if scoring big runs thick and fast is on the agenda and you need to wind the bat up and give a full follow through of the bat and hit through the ball with power and hit 4s and 6s – you have to use the parallel method.

So use the sequential method in test cricket or when you are fresh to the crease and use the parallel method if it is one-day cricket and your arms, wrists and hands are sufficiently warmed up enough and adept enough to make the adjustment for the swinging ball and the changing line.

You must be a master at using both methods of picking line if you are to go on to play for the country and you must know which method to adopt under varying circumstances. If you pick the wrong method for any given condition or circumstance then you will be in big trouble – so just follow the brief guide we have given you above to decide.

The ideal situation is to get your body into position by z-point and pick both line AND length by this point and prime yourself up for a big shot, but what if the ball is swinging erratically? Then this method may prove to bring about your

---

[13] This was one of the biggest plus points to Tendulkar's batting – playing the ball late and using the wrists to generate batspeed.

downfall! It all depends on how quickly your hands and wrists can react when and if the ball deviates from its initial path it was at by the z-point time.

The general rule of thumb is to pick length as quickly as possible and pick line as late as possible but not too late. However we can successfully pick line both ealier **OR** later than that which we have advocated in the diagram above. Inspect the following diagram:

Diagram 30: pick the line earlier OR later

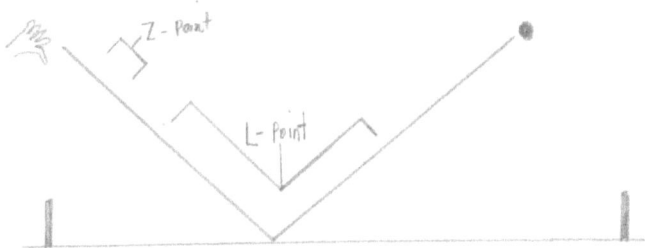

So we see in the diagram that the line can be picked both earlier **AND** later. This is the zone or time by which line can permissably be picked without creating probelms. But no earlier and no later! There is a reason for this – not picking line too early or too late that is. If we pick the line too early the ball might deviate more and we end up playing the wrong line and if we pick the line too late it might get through our defences by that point and we would, yes, have picked the line but would not have enough time to react and make the physical movement necessary to actuall play the ball.

To deploy a method which successfully allows you to pick, judge and get into position early enough to play the line of the ball is one of the most **CRITICAL** facets to batting and is something which must be honed and developed through rigourous practice in the nets. You must practice using both methods whilst conducting your training routine as come match day you may be required to interchangeably switch from the two methods which exist, and it is important you appreciate why you **MUST** learn them and why you **MUST** practice them in order to be the front line specialist batter your dreaming of becoming and go on to play for the counrty.

So just remember to use this little trick in regards to picking line in your favour and use it to make the bowler's life more difficult and make your life of either scoring fast easier or not getting out easier.

CHAPTER 19
Use that bottom hand!

There is a lot of coaching and guidance in regard the grip a batter should adopt which is not as complicated as coaches make it out to be. You simply pick up the bat in your hands, position your top hand such that there is no hyperflexion in either direction and place your bottom hand so it is centred and there is also no hyperflexion. Especially in regard to the top hand grip the hand **MUST** grip somehwere in between hyperflexion inwards towards the forearm and hyperflexion outwards where the top of the hand is facing the top of the forearm – it must be somewhere inbetween this and feel comfortable whilst you are conducting the swing of the arms and the straight follow through with the arms. If it were bent inwards, the top hand that is, then we would have trouble playing our off side strokes and if it were bent outwards we would have trouble playing our onside strokes[14]. This is the theory behind gripping the bat properly.

A similar thing applies to the bootom hand grip. We want it to be centred so we can play our offside **AND** onside shots comfortably.

Contrary to popular belief it is not the top hand which guides the stroke and creates power or facilitates the ability to play

---

[14] Try holding the bat with the top hand in both hyperflexed positions and note how uncomfortable it feels.

front foot and back foot defense, but rather is the bottom hand! The bottom hand does all the work and can be considered the *'actuator'* whilst both defensive and attacking strokeplay is concerned.

So don't get entangled with the seeming complexity of the subject of how to hold and grip the bat – it is actually very straightforward and simple.[15]

We don't want to lead with the top hand and allow the top hand to do all the work and hit through the line of the ball but rather want to lead with a nice high elbow and allow the bottom hand to assist in dveloping bat speed and direction to our stroke. Yes, the bottom hand has very little if anything to do with our ability to strike the ball the way we wish – it is just there to actually hold on to the bat but is as such critical in our ability to play defense **OR** attack.

The majority of problems which happen in batting technique is where the batter is trying to use the top hand to hit through the line and generate batspeed as opposed to leading with the elbow and getting the elbow nice and high and **THEN** using the top hand as what you could call to a minor extent a placement generator. So the top hand has proportionately

---

[15] We don't have to put the bat on the ground and hold it in a V shape form. This is an aspect of cricket which has been over-coached and must be obliterated from the idea of of teaching someone how to hold a bat!

little to do with how well we can strike and hit the ball – perhaps only merely as a ditrection and placement acquirer.[16]

The bottom hand is the actuator like we just said. It aids in playing drives, pulls, cuts, hooks, flicking the ball, lofting the ball over the infield, playing front foot defense and driving on the up. The only time the bottom hand dominance is not required is when we playing back foot defense. It is with the bottom hand that we are able to generate batspeed and actually forcefully strike at the ball. Also whilst playing forward defense it aids us in accurately and perfectly presenting the full face of the bat to the ball. The top hand, unlike what many coaches are trying to tell you, is almost meaningless in our quest of playing defense and attack in a game of cricket.

The bottom hand must be as active and precise as possible especially when playing the flick through the onside and driving on gthe rise. These shots, and many more as we have just outlined above, cannot be played and executed without the force and power generated by the bottom hand. Yes, cricket is almost the same and very similar to baseball where the bottom hand is everything and is relied upon to hit the ball harder and longer and with more placement and accuracy.

---

[16] Even then, it is the bottom hand which aids in placement and ditrection!

The biggest examples of this bottom hand dominance which leads to more power and batspeed is Sir Vivian Richards and Sachin Tendulkar. Both were power hitters and wanted to strike the ball with as much force as possible and relied upon the bottom hand in almost all of their strokes.

So the motto to be understood is that we should lead with a nice high elbow, allow the hands to come through second and lastly use the bottom hand to direct and place the ball with power and force whether it be a cut shot or a straight drive. It is the bottom hand which is the actuator in batting and allows you to play good forceful cricket as well as present the full face of the bat whilst playing forward defense.

The biggest thing you will have to practice is using the bottom hand in tandem with the wrists to flick the ball through the onside.[17]

"The top hand does NOT allow us to generate batspeed and power in our shots but rather the bottom hand. Always lead with the elbow and let the hands come second and then the bat third"

..........Nikhil & Co

---

[17] This was one of tendulkar's trademark shots

"Do NOT try to lead with the top hand and arm in attempt to hit through the line of the ball. Always use the elbows and the bottom hand"
…………...*Nikhil & Co*

It is all about the elbow, hands and bat sequence or chain of events which lies at the crux of good batting. Each must happen in the right order and care must be taken that we **DON'T** use the top hand as part of the hands part of this routine, but rather use the bottom hand. Effectively the top hand is *'dead'* in this routine which allows for good orthodox batting and is only there to hold the bat – we can't hold the bat with one hand can we?

Aim to be a strong bottom hand player like Tendulkar, Viv, Nathan Astle and Chris Gayle and remember the bottom hand is everything in batting. Start developing the wristiness in your shots along side the power and force which bottom hand batting facilitates.

And remember what we said about how to hold the bat – don't worry or believe in those trying to over-coach the way to hold the bat but instead use what feels comfortable once you take your guard and setup.[18]

Especially in one-day cricket where hitting boundaries is of utmost importance, acquiring the expertise in and attain mastery

---

[18] Viv and tendulkar never put the bat on the floor and formed two 'V's' with their hands so why should you! Batting is a deep subject matter and we don't have time to waste on over-coaching how to hold the bat.

over using the bottom hand to not only generate power but direction to your shots cannot be stressed enough. Being flexible and agile in regards to being able to adjust and maneuver the exact grip and hold of the bottom hand is a priceless asset in batting and as we said is as such the 'actuator' in the whole act of batting per say.

Like we said the bottom hand is used in every single shot except the back foot defense. This is because there is no power or direction being demanded within this shot and per say all's we have to do is get over the ball and let it hit a dead bat and let the ball fall to the ground. If we were to use the bottom hand whilst playing back foot defense then the force of the bottom hand may allow the ball to pop up and if the ball steeples and bounces higher we would be in big trouble – had we used a strong bottom hand grip that is. So in back foot defense it is the top hand which is the *'actuator'* and not the bottom hand. Do not use the bottom hand in back foot defense in case the ball steeples and grows on you and you cant get on top of and over it which may in most cases lead to you being forced to allow the ball to hit the bat with your bottom hand tightly gripped. In this scenario you will almost always pop up a catch to the close in fielder.

So in conclusion, the bottom hand is everything in batting and is considered the 'actuator' of all defensive **AND** attacking shots and one can generate tremondous batspeed with the bottom hand and a flick of the wrists alone – just like Tenudlkar did! Do not underestimate the impact and difference matering the manouveuring of the bottom hand is going to have on your batting, and don't listen to coaches and the likes when they say that the top hand leads and that the top hand creates power and direction in your shots – this is a fallacy!

CHAPTER 20
BECOMING THE SPEARHEAD OF THE FAST BOWLING ATTACK:

Amongst the most athletic and demanding acts within the field of sports in general, fast bowling is considered the ultimate crowd puller, and a perfectly legitimate task for one to aspire towards. The aim of fast bowling is to beat the batsman with sheer pace as well as swing and deviation off the pitch, and is an act which is adorned and loved and attempted by almost every cricketing enthusiast whether it be a street cricketer or a professional or aspiring professional. It is well known that Tendulkar himself also wanted to be a fast bowler and have that aggression and hot bloodedness which fast bowling is often associated with.

Certain elements to fast bowling which are crucial and in totality make for an effective if not great fast bowler must be there, and they are:

- Raw pace
- Slower ball
- Inswinger
- Outswinger
- Deviation off the seam
- Bounce
- Generating pace off just a short run
- Accuracy

The ultimate facet which ultimately decides whether you will be selected for the country does not come down to raw pace but rather swing and deviation off the seam. Also generating extreme pace off just a short run like Wasim Akram to be exact. Wasim Akram was the greatest fast bowler ever to play the game as he had and possessed in his lair, all the qualities mentioned above.

What separates an average fast bowler to a great one and what separates the state level fast bowler to the national level one? It is simply the combination of raw pace and swing. Yes, the other factors are important but to even catch the eyes of a district level selector, one must exhibit this potential – the potential for raw pace **AND** swing that is. In reality and at the end of the day, the rest can be taught and acquired but the potential must be there in the first place. Kapil Dev is also another example of a bowler who had the raw pace and swing to catch the selector's eyes and be in serious contention for national selection.

The slower ball, accuracy, and deviation off the seam is something which can be taught if mentored and guided by a knowledgeable fast bowling coach; however, it is the raw pace and swing which cannot. One must be of a minimum height in order to generate a decent and proper bounce – say 5'7" to 5'8" to be exact. So this is one thing which cannot be taught – you are either tall enough or you are not!

In an ideal world a fast bowler should create an illusion for the batsman which makes picking the pace and length of the ball that much harder. This is achieved by coming in off a shorter run and having the capacity to let the shoulder and upper body explode at point of release – making for a ball which travels much faster than the batsman would have predicted or anticipated. The perfect exponent of this was Wasim Akram and this is the very reason he was so great.

See, to get quality batsman out there must be deviation in the form of seam movement or lateral ways movement in the form of swing.

Without these elements one is just wasting his time. So the key requisite requirements to bowl fast for the country are being tall enough, having the raw pace and the ability to get the ball to move in the air in the form of the out swinger and in swinger – the rest can be taught!

There are many bowlers who come in off a big run so it isn't to say that you have to have the abiity to create an illusion for the batsman in the form of a short run-up and exploding at release. It is only a nicety and an ideal – there are many bowlers who have enjoyed success at the international level without this idea of creating an illusion for the batsman, so you don't have to be a Wasim Akram to succeed but you **DO** have to be like Wasim Akram if you want to be a great.

So if you have the height, pace and swing then it is well worth your while to hone and fine tune your bowling such that you can be considered for national selection, but without these 3 components it is sorry to say that you are just wasting your time. Ajit Agarkar of India was only 5'7" tall yet had the swing and movement in the air and off the pitch and pace and was one of India's if not the world's best fast bowler and even broke the one-day record of being the fastest bowler to reach 50 wickets in one-day cricket to further attest to the fact that swing and seam movement combined with a certain minimum height is all it takes to bowl fast for your country.

Accuracy, seam movement and the slower ball can be taught within a matter of weeks, but the raw pace and swing is innate and you either have it or you don't. As Kapil Dev said: ***"God gave me the out-swinger, I had to work on the rest."*** So do a bit of self evaluation and reflecting to see where you stand and whether it is worth your while to pursue fast bowling, as fast bowling is very competitive and you don't want to waste your time attempting something you just cannot succeed at on a higher level of cricket where the batsman are so good.

So if looking for someone to emulate than by all means watch and learn from the great Wasim Akram and if you have it in you, attempt to come in off a short run and explode at point of release just like Akram did. We are talking about a bowler who was not just great but almost superhuman, and you needn't be that good to realistically aim for national selection.

The smooth and right length of run up followed by an explosiveness at point of release is what it is going to take. The longer your run up is the better chance the batsman gets to gauge the momentum you are generating and better foresee the exact pace on the ball you will be putting. Once great batsmen get a feel for your rhythm and how fast the ball comes out the hand in comparison to how long your run up is, it becomes all the more difficult to beat them for sheer pace. Wasim Akram had it all! He had the raw pace **AND** the inswinger/outswinger. So coming in off a long run doesn't mean its all over and dusted for you as an aspiring fast bowler, but it just means that you will have to generate deviation or lateral ways movement in addition to the pace if you are to get these guys out – elite batsman that is.

CHAPTER 21
CAN YOU BECOME A GREAT SPIN BOWLER?

There are average spinners then there are good spinners and then there are great spinners. What distinguishes amongst these categories? Well, there are a few defining features of spin bowling which ideally must be there for you to be in the great category, and they are:

- Top spinner
- Googly/dusra
- Pin-point accuracy
- Flipper/arm ball
- Using the crease
- Subtle changes in flight
- Setting the batsman up via pre deliveries
- Subtle changes in run up

These various aspects of spin bowling, which when combined, in totality reverberate and give forth to what we would call the perfect spin bowler. There have only been 4 perfect spin bowlers in the history of cricket and they were: Warne, Kumble, Murali and Harbhajan Singh.

They were perfect because in addition to the skills mentioned above they had the mental acumen and guile, deception and artistry which others did not! To be in contention to get wickets against batsman at the national level you must possess each and every skill aforementioned and yes, spin bowling is a hard trade to master but the ranks are full of aspiring and enthusiastic spin bowlers, particularly in India, and the selectors have a large pool of people and spinners to select from. So if you serious about playing national level then you must work on your game and everything and every nuance related to spin bowling. Just like fast bowling, spin bowling is highly competitive and it is only those who have actually mastered the art and acquired and honed the specifics skills to a nicety who get considered for selection. There is no place or position for the spinner who doesn't possess these attributes to great spin bowling which we have listed above, and there is no easy way or sneaking in through the back door when we talk about national selection. The exact and thorough treatment of spin bowling and what it takes and how to do it are postulated and explained within our book titled: *'The science, strategy and secrets behind the heroes of spin bowling'*, which we recommend as an **ABSOLUTE** must read for the serious spinner.

For now just remember that in addition to the core skills of spin bowling there is a certain guile, deception and artistry necessitated whilst bowling to the best batsman in the world and that in spin bowling one must tactfully lure or setup the batsman as oppose to beating him outright with sheer spin or lateral ways movement.

The mental component of the spin bowling trade is somewhat a large subject domain and we encourage you to read our book on spin bowling which takes approximately 150 pages or 2 hours to teach you all the street smarts and mental acumen and shrewdness you will need to be selected for the country.

The book is co-authored by the great Rajinder Goel, leading wicket taker of India's domestic Ranji trophy competition and myself a state level legspinner from Australia, and is foreworded by Wayne Spratford – a sport scientist for the Australian Cricket Board, PhD in the biomechanics of spin bowling and lecturer within the sport science discipline.

CHAPTER 22
BECOMING A GOOD FIELDER:

Being a fielder comes down to two things physical athleticism and agility **AND** mental proficiency and perceptiveness. What does this mean exactly – mental proficiency and perceptiveness that is?

Well it comes down to and centers around this idea from physics called vector forces, which yes is more pertinent and relevant to batting, but it is also of material consequence in the act of fielding as well.[19] Reading vector forces and watching the ball's bounce off the pitch and the batsman's initial movements gives us as fielders vital clues as to what to do! Which way to go that is, to the left or to the right or lunging upwards into the air or even picking the ball off the ground and throwing at the stumps.

This is all mental and is we said revolves around the understanding and application of vector forces whilst we are in our fielding position, which ultimately dictates what we are going to do **IN ADVANCE**. This is the whole fundamental principle behind being a good fielder – knowing your movements in advance and before the bat-ball contact even happens. Also we can rely on information about ball-pitch contact to guide us as well – guide us as to whether we will be lunging in the air or diving forward along the ground or going to the left or the right and so on and so forth.

Some of the best fielders in the world were Jonty Rhodes, Mark Waugh, Ricky Ponting, Azharuddin, Yuvraj Singh and now

---

[19] You MUST read the other books especially the 1st one: *'The mind and method of an elite cricketer'*, to get a proper and exact grip on what vector forces are!

Ravindra Jadeja. The most crucial fielding positions in cricket usually are point, cover and square leg. It is within these positions that fielders are keenly watching the ball beyond and after z-point and also watching the feet work and back lift of the batsman to get an idea of which way the batter might hit the ball – it could be either to his right or to his left or along the ground or in the air. The fielder is watching for the vector force generated when the batsman glides his bat and hands through the ball and is eagerly awaiting to anticipate going either left off his right foot or right off his left foot.

Depending on if the ball was pitched up or pitched short a fielder may know when to begin a lunge in the air before or just after the ball deflects off the bat or similarly when to prepare to collect the moving ball off the ground and throw at the stumps. The best fielders are the ones who are looking out for and anticipating these vector forces both out the bowler's hand and off the pitch as well as the vector force generated when the ball hits the bat or bat hits the ball.

For example, if the fielder is at point and sees the batsman get behind the ball and not play away from his body, then he can conclude the ball will be hit through covers or forward of point – and can begin bouncing off his left foot to move rightwards. If he sees the ball pitched a little short, he can conclude the ball may not be hit along the ground and prepare to lunge skyward for a catch. If he sees the ball pitched up than he can conclude a drive along the ground is probable and begin bouncing off his left foot as soon as possible to stop the ball at forward of point area.

These are some common examples of the implications of vector forces to fielders on a cricket field, and the way in which they save runs, get catches and complete runouts and all through a superior understanding and application of vector forces.

Second is the actual physical component which makes for a good fielder. The fielder must have good overall athleticism and be able to jump high, dive with an outstretched arm, be nimble and sharp on their feet, and be able to change direction via the use of sharp footwork and foot coordination. Also, being able to catch one handed and your running speed along with the ability to throw the ball long and accurately constitutes the key skills which are required of one to be classed in the great fielder category. Your catching skills should be sharp and you should have the agility and accuracy to collect the moving ball off the ground and throw at the stumps and hit them to ultimately effect the run-out opportunity.

If you are fielding out in the deep or on the boundary or in close proximity, then you must have a *'strong arm'* and be able to throw the ball to the keeper straight back over the bails/stumps consistently. Your main job as a fielder is to **NOT** drop catches and effect runout opportunities. The other skills are important, yes, but these are the most critical ones so to speak.

So you now know that there is indeed a science behind fielding just like batting and bowling, and should have an appreciation for what it will take in order to be a good one. It all comes down to practice, physical fitness and agility and of course the mental presence to observe point of release from bowler's hand, ball-pitch contact **AND** ball-bat contact. Like we said this will come from a proper and competent understanding of what a vector is. This is explained in the father book to these sequel books called: *'The Mind & Method of an Elite cricketer'*.

So, this is what it will take to become a good fielder and is something even the batsman and bowlers should endeavor to master. Being a good fielder could may well be the difference between you being selected in the team and not. Fielding is critical in one-day cricket and if you can save 15-20 runs in the field and effect run outs and take difficult catches, then there is every chance you will be picked in then team ahead of the next guy.

CHAPTER 23
WHY CAPTAINCY IS SO IMPORTANT:

The captain is only as good as his players and their potential, or as is often said an army can only be as strong as its regiment – this is true and must be accepted, but good leadership, planning & strategy go a long way and can make all the difference in how well your troops perform on the day. As well as charisma and tactile leadership, these are the qualities and traits along with good fielding, which add up to form what is known as *'out cricket'*.

Try to realize and actualize the full potential of your bowling unit and your batting unit by being tactile, versatile and flexible along with being prepared and following a plan. Also having back up plans pre-seeded in case of any contingencies and if things don't go according to plan. Good captaincy is not just about marshaling your men but is highly sensitive to and dependent upon what is known as *'out-cricket'*. Out-cricket pertains to things such as structuring your batting order, bowling the right bowler at the right time, choosing the right time to bring the spinner on, good effective fielding and field placements, making the right decision upon winning the toss which will yield an optimal performance by your batting and bowling units, rotating the strike to give the in-form batsman more strike and possession of the strike, making it clear what exactly you expect from your batters and bowlers, showing a positive body language to your team and last but not least maintaining a good optimistic relationship full of positive exchanges and words of encouragement to your bowlers.

These are the things which good captaincy is about and, yes, marshaling your men or troops as if you were a captain in an army does count for something, however, it is the harnessing of your horses or the talent you have on the team which is of most critical and pivotal significance and the main requisite skill you should have as a captain who wants to captain the country.

As a captain, you must do the little things right or more fittingly, you must do everything right. From batting and bowling orders to field placements and wicket taking tactics to containing the scoring rate tactics, everything must be done right and be *'on song'* as they say in cricket. Generally, but not necessarily always, try to restrict the scoring rate by setting the 6-3 field and making it clear to your bowlers where you want them to pitch – either off stump or leg stump, and don't be afraid to bring on the spinner if you are being dominated and hit around as the spinner is potentially the most potent wicket taker known to the game of cricket.

Bring on your in-form bowler first to open the bowling as the potency of getting wickets early and its ability to impact the outcome of the game is at its peak in the first 0-7 overs – there is no point bringing on your wicket taking in-form bowler at the end or at the death and getting wickets at the end, is there? This will not leverage any sort of advantage toward victory like taking the wickets early on. If you can take say 3 -4 wickets early on then this gives you a whopping prospect and probability of winning the game. Once and wherein you take early wickets and shift the momentum and tempo your way the pressure is then completely on the batting side and you as a bowling side need only bowl sensibly and contain the runs to restrict the total to one which is easily chase able. Cricket is a team sport and the bowlers are there to make life easier for their batsmen and the batsmen are there to make life easier for their bowlers. Make it clear as a captain that you expect a good performance from your bowlers and even if you can't do what is ideal and that is to take 3-4 wickets early, then you should at least try restrict the total by some 20-25 runs and make the batters' life easier.

It is a common ploy in all forms of cricket to use the spinner as a weapon or a wild card when you need to break the partnership. In fact the spinner is your ultimate go-to man in highly competitive contested matches as they can be so dangerous if they are accurate enough and know how and when to use the variation ball. Actively seek out a good leg spinner from your state or area and try to groom him up for the state or country. Spin bowling has a huge mental component and is more mental than physical and you need only offer the right coaching and mentoring to the budding youngster to mold a champion out of a child. If a spinner shows ability to turn the ball and can bowl all the variation balls and shows a good potentiality for bowling the slower higher loopier one, then scout him straight away and begin grooming him in the mental aspects of the trade. These mental aspects are 70% of being a champion spinner and can be easily taught and inculcated within the youngster via the imparting of some simple principles as well as finer points about the discipline of spin bowling per say.

You must consult formally with the coach to decide the optimal batting order and the batting order which can result in as bigger total as possible. It is important here to not let your big hitters and power hitters come in too late as this would mean you are essentially wasting their skills and not giving them enough of the overs to do their job, which is to hit boundaries and secure as bigger total as possible. So generally the batting order goes in ascending order with your biggest and most powerful hitters coming in first. There is also a theory to play percentage cricket at the start and merely accumulate runs risk free and then accelerate towards the end with your power hitters, but there are 6-8 competent batsman in the team so why wait to launch an onslaught and score as bigger total as possible. In one day cricket, send your powerful big hitter in as soon as is possible and feasible.

One tactic you can try is to use one of your openers to simply rotate the strike and stay at the crease and simply accumulate runs slowly and steadily while the other opener goes all out for the big runs. The reasoning for this tactic is to use the sheet anchor opener to beat and knock the shine off the ball and make the task of hitting big for the middle order batsmen so much easier as the ball is softer and wont swing as much. Also to prevent a collapse at the top of the order. At the end of the day these approaches are more useful and applicative in 50 over cricket and not so much Test cricket as one-day cricket is abound by certain constraints and you only have 50 overs to *'show your stuff'*, so to speak. Even if you have a collapse or a semi collapse you still have competent enough batters from number 5-8 to get the runs.

Not only do you have to give your bowlers the right fields but you have to pick and choose which man will field in which position based on how agile and talented a fielder they are. Determine with the bowler where exactly the run saving positions are and where exactly the catching fielder might be and put your best fielders there. This is a classic example of harnessing your horse – giving the bowler your best fielders in the crucial run saving and catching positions.

So being captain is not as simple as just marshalling your troops and leading them and governing them as though you were a colonel for an army, but rather, is more about doing your part in using strategy, tactics and cleverness to get the best possible result from the bowler's attempts to bowl well. Also to optimize the total by strategically deciding upon the batting order.

The best captainship in cricket was the 1992 world cup final where Imran Khan lead his men beautifully and harnessed his horses beautifully. He knew just the right time when to use which bowler and when. His premier fast bowler and most dangerous bowler on the team, Wasim Akram, was given specific instructions to bowl his fastest and was brought on at the right time to pick up the 3 crucial wickets at the end which sealed the game and victory for Pakistan. Imran had saved a good 2-4 overs for wasim Akram, the premium act of fast bowling ever to live, to come in at the death and secure the win.

You don't have to rule with an iron fist but you need to have the courage and gallantry to put your foot down and decide what is best for the team without letting any individual's own opinions and own perceptions of the game to get in the way. You are captain and perceiving and interpreting the game is your job and harnessing your horse is your job not the batters or bowlers job – their job is to simply perform the role they have been assigned to do and do whatv they have been instructed to do and nothing more.

As captain the onus and will to lead and instruct your troops gallantly and with chivalry is on you and you are the boss and to some extent accountable for the team's success or failure.

By harnessing your horse so to speak, you can improve your performance in one-day cricket by as much as 30% - 50%, so be circumspect and vigilant about your responsibilities as captain and leader of the team.

So a captain must have the charisma and cricketing foresight to harness his horses for the best possible outcome and at the national level this is the very element or trait in a captain the selectors are looking for. Further, he must have the gallantry via both a positive body language on the field as well as being emotive, diplomatic and protective of his troops in front of the media if he is to be deserved of the role of captain for the country.

The subject of captaincy can get quite complex as there is so many variables and possibilities a captain must weigh up, juggle and consider before he moves forward with a particular decision or plan. This skill, knowing how to harness your horse that is, is something which comes with experience however is essentially based around theory and theoretical premise. So once again we just cannot ignore the science when it comes to the game of cricket as even the captain's job is somewhat a rather multiplex, methodical and scientific task.

Approaching your captaincy with clinical precision and having insight as well as courage to make brave and sometimes compromising decisions is what makes a good captain, and is a job which usually only goes to the man with the most knowledge about the game but also charisma and leadership qualities.

CHAPTER 24
BECOMING A COMPETENT WICKET KEEPER:

A wicket keeper's view down the pitch is similar to that of the batsman and your job is similar to that of a batsman in that you must be reading the ball's length and judging it's final path once it bounces, including and accounting for any longitudinal or lateral ways movement which may happen. The difficult aspect of keeping is when you are keeping to the spinners. It is here where you need to really be reading his flatter ones, his loopier ones and variations in amount of turn being generated and keeping your hand positions either high or low. When you see the top spinner or loopier one you must immediately get your hands nice and high. When you see the flatter one or faster one you must position your hands low and be prepared to bring them slightly higher after the z-point of the ball in case there is an edge.

Based on the sideways movement being generated by the bowler and the way you see a particular ball shaping up, you must be prepared to either take off from the left foot towards the right for leg spinner or be balanced on both feet if the ball goes straight or comes in like an offspinner. But the main thing for you keepers is to know when to lift your hands up high for the one which bounces a bit more and keep them low when the ball is expected to skid through or stay low.

When keeping to the pacers just remember to read the ball up until z-point to determine and accurately guess whether the ball will move inwards or outwards and be ready to bounce off either your left or right foot to move in the other direction.

So position of the hands and which foot to bounce off from is the key for you keepers. Reading the spinner's loopy one or bouncy one is important too.

So this is the core skills set required of a wicket keeper to be in contention for national selection, and as you now know, is all about reading the vector forces being imparted on the ball. So in a sense a wicket keeper is also a worthy and perfectly valid athlete in the scheme of sports in general as he is using bodily movement **AND** mental acumen in the form of picking and reading the vector forces being imparted on the ball to perform his role.

Usually to gain a spot as a wicketkeeper in the team you should know how to bat also. The ability to lunge out and dive and take one handed catches really impresses when you are chasing a wicket keeping position in the team and the more physically agile you are the better. But like we said, most wicket keepers are good batsman and that's how they gain selection into the country's team.

So to keep wickets for your country you must be good with your hands, nimble on your feet, able to dive and lunge, take catches one handed, read the spinner's variation balls and last but not least, read the vector forces being imparted on the ball. These are the main ingredients of what makes a national level wicket keeper.

CHAPTER 25
BATTING AT THE HIGHEST LEVEL

Millions of people play cricket both at a leisurely level as well as a serious district, club or state level but there are only few limited spots available in the national team. What and who decides whether a batsman will get picked for the country and go on to become a professional? What is the difference between a professional and a semi professional or amateur? A professional athlete in any sport including cricket is one who can consistently score runs, make big scores and do so consistently under any condition, circumstance or variable; and whats more, a professional knows what it will take to outsmart and outwit his opponent and successfully pile on the runs no matter what the encumbering or adverse pressures and situations may be.

See, to become a professional and represent the country you must do a plethora and range of certain things right and in a certain way – a way which the semi-professional or amateur cannot. You must have the fortitude and prowess to do things right and get the result. This result for you batsman out there is to score runs and keep your wicket intact for as long as possible without letting the run-rate slide – which when taken within context of the fact that cricket is a tough sport, is something easier said than done! This is what is meant by classing a batsman into the professional category. Further, the batsman must have the aptness and fitness to perform in big match situations and under extreme pressure. This is the difference between the professional batsman and the non – professional batsman, and the one who goes on to play for the country and the one who does not!

Like we said, a batsman may look perfectly competent and capable in the nets but does he have what it takes to size up and adjust to the pitch on live match day? Does he have the capacity to play 3-5 different strokes to the same ball? Does he have the innings building skills to not give away his wicket cheaply against the swinging ball? Does he know how to get a sighter the risk free way and once and wherein settled accelerate the run rate? Does he know how to consistently find the gaps? Does he have the ability to play 'baseball' and bludgeon the ball for sixes? Does he know how to score 360^0 around the pitch and use deft touch and finesse when required to deflect the ball behind the wicket? These are all aspects to batting which the professional batsman takes very seriously and ensures and guarantees that he can perform in front of any situation. This is what it takes to play higher level and representative level cricket and be classed in the *'professional category'*.

Who were some of the batsman of the pre-modern era who when you watched them play you would immediately think *"this guy is a professional"?* There were many such as Tendulkar, Viv Richards, Steve waugh, Brian Lara, Aravinda Desilva and so on. But the point to be drilled home is that the serious and professional batter takes pride in having a superior grip over the science behind batting and the ability to perform under pressure which the amateur does **NOT**.[20]

The professional batsman takes his practice routine as well as preparation routine very seriously. Everything must be practiced and honed in for big match day and he shouldn't be found wanting

---

[20] Aravinda De Silva's 107* in the final of WC1996 was one of the most mature and professional exhibition of batting you may ever see.

for a mere lack in mental toughness and preparation and get out cheaply. Rather, the professional batsman puts a very high price on his wicket and does not surrender so easily and to just average bowling. It takes a bowling of a very high standard and a special delivery and whatsmore the ability to set up and lure the batsman to get the professional batsman out.

The professional batsman takes his journey of learning and engraining the deeper science behind batting very seriously and does not foster a deaf ear to those around him who are giving him advice as to how to improve his game, but rather leaves an open ear to any piece of advice and wisdom which comes his way.

The biggest trait of the professional is have the patience to learn the hidden science behind batting to his utmost ability and learning from your mistakes and not repeating the same mistake again and again. Pro batters are **ALWAYS** prepared. What does this mean? Well it simply means that they have ascertained the conditions, the pitch, the strengths and weaknesses of the opposing teams bowlers and will simply **NOT** let being a little mentally tough and prepared let them down. Preparation and becoming familiar with the ensuing conditions on big match day can mean the difference between winning and losing, and professional batsmen **KNOW** this!

The professional batsman understands what is required of him and what it will take to achieve it and will do anything and everything in his power to create a leverage toward victory for his team.

Another crucial aspect of being a professional batsman is to carry and stock a range of different bats suited and especially crafted for certain pitches. As no two pitches in cricket are the same. The most important thing for professional batsman is to have the right bat for any particular pitch. For example if the pitch is keeping low than you want a lower middle or sweet spot and if the pitch is bouncy and lively you want a higher middle or sweet spot.

Taking guard is also important and the professional batsman never makes the mistake of taking a sub-optimal guard.[21] The little sighter period at the start of a batsman's innings can mke or break the batter's hopes of getting a score and professional batsman know this! They are very meticulous about the way in which they conduct there little sighter period and do so in the most scientific fashion possible. There is this thing called the 3 – layered approach to getting a sighter which you will come to know via reading the Tendulkar book, and its implications for a professional batsman are absolutely collossal and it is absolutely critical you read the tendulkar book to be taught what exactly this 3-layered approach to getting a sighter is about. [22]

The most important skill to have when talking about being a professional batter is your visual accuity and following the prescribed method shown prior within the book. You must have a system or a method which allows you to accurately and consistently distinguish between a good ball and a bad ball. Further, how you are going to negotiate anything which falls within the confines of the c-box. Also knowing how and which foot to play your defensive stroke – back or front. Footwork lays the foundation, or in most cases at least, for a batter to actually get

---

[21] Virat Kohli WC2019 semi final Vs NZ. Kohli takes the orthodox middle stup guard when the ball was swinging into the pads and he needed take a leg or middle and leg stump guard

[22] Because we are mainly introducing and defining the core skills required to play professional cricket in this book, we will not be teaching the nuances to this 3-layered approach within this book.

into position to hit the ball where he wants to hit it, and cant be stressed enough that you follow the teachings within this and our other books in regard the foot work approach or methodology you must hone to become an attacking and exuberant batsman. We call this the Tendulkar method, which Viv Richards and Mark Waugh also used to adopt[23]. There is no time to be scared of the ball and go back as your trigger movement! If you are to stroke the ball with power and play attacking cricket then your trigger movement **MUST** be forward. You see, to play for the country and that too to be a great, you must lean into the ball and attempt to hit through the line. Also to hit across the line by flicking the wrists at the last moment.

The second most important skill for a batsman to hone whilst training for professional status is to have 3-5 different strokes up his sleeve to any particular ball landing in the same spot. This then puts the batsman in the chooser category and **NOT** the beggar category.[24]

A fine defensive technique is absolutely **MUST** for the aspiring professional batsman, and in fact should be mastered 1st and before you start practicing actually hitting the ball long and far or playing run scoring shots. There is a whole book titled *'Playing the length ball like Bradman'* which is only 112 pages long which explicitly guides you through the nuances and finer points of defensive

---

[23] Sculpting **YOU** to be the next master batsman: Sachin Tendulkar MUST be read for you to appreciate the footwork required of a pro batsman.

[24] This comes from hours of practice in the nets practicing playing different shots to the exact same line and length!

technique and what is required of you to keep your wicket intact and stay at the crease longer. **Please read this book!**

CHAPTER 26
BOWLING AT THE HIGHEST LEVEL

Sometimes just bowling a good ball and that's it is not good enough in competitive professional level cricket, or any form of cricket for that matter. For example you might get the ball to swing too far and miss the edge of the bat or you might bowl a beautiful yorker and contain the scoring rate of the batsman or you might get the batsman setup for the wicket taking ball through a sequence of pre deliveries and bowl it inaccurately or you may bowl your wicket taking ball too early and not have the batsman properly 'lulled' so to speak to offer the wrong shot to the wrong ball. We call this in umbrella terms **'Bowling with a plan and not bowling blindly'**.

It is most cases in professional cricket that the bowling of the variation ball with pin point accuracy is the one which gets you that wicket you were toiling away for, and hence it cant be stressed enough that you bowling your variation balls and having control over their trajectory and line and length as though you have the ball on a string, so to speak.

All this equates to the fact that professional bowling demands of you skill and guile but most of all accuracy and the ability to use your wicket taking ball at the right time. Another thing which the professional bowler takes with utmost seriousness is having a plan to each batsman based on his past performances/strengths/weaknesses and patterns of scoring.

Keep your fitness levels up so you don't tire and can bowl at peak levels for the duration of the game stretch and warm up before games so your limbs are supple and flexible. Especially stretch the groin as the team can't afford to have you walk off the field with a strained groin muscle.

Remember, be accurate with your wicket taking ball and that all it takes is 2 inches of lateral ways movement to have your man back in the pavillion. Sometimes swinging or spinning the ball too far is good but sometimes it is not. The professional bowler acknowledges this fact and incorporates into his strategy regards getting a highly training and honed batsman out.

Get used to the idea of bowling with a plan and gradually 'lulling' or setting the batsman up for the final wicket taking ball – this is the only way you are going to get the professional batsman out. This game cricket is a tough sport, yes, but is easily mastered and honed by even the common district cricketer. If you are to distinguish yourself from the pack then you must have the street smarts and the cricketing brain to do so. This is all mental and it is 100% true that cricket indeed is the great mental game and that you give yourself a grounding in the mental acumen required of you by reading all of our books carefully and patiently. We will teach you everything you just have to read and follow on. We have done the hard work of critically analysing the mind and method required in cricket and subsequently providing tips and advice based on science and not guestimation. All's you need do is follow on to the books and we can

GUARANTEE that you will improve your cricket and your game at an exponential rate – some 30% - 60% overnight.

The next thing professional bowlers deploy to get wickets is by tactile and strategic field placements and cleverly decieving the batsman both physically and mentally. This is shown in our other book titled: 'The science, strategy & secrets of the heroes of spin bowling – Warne, Kumble, Murali & Harbhajan.

A zippy snappy action combined with the variation ball(s) is what makes a bowler successful at the highest level. Some examples of this are Wasim Akram, Shane Warne, Muralitharan and Jasprit Bumrah jut to name a few of the key ones.

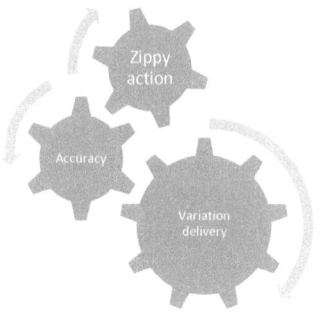

CHAPTER 27
TEST CRICKET BATTING MODE VS ONEDAY BATTING MODE

The reality is that both forms of the game are equally as important in the real world which seeks both excitement, showmanship and an exhilerating viewing experience as well as an the opportunity to appreciate the skills and cababilities of the professional cricketer – on a more technical level that's is. Or in other words, the knowledgeable fan and spectator endears and adorns the opportunity to see a professional athlete in motion and view exactly how he contends with the situation at hand and just how worthy he is of an exemplary status within the keen and endearing cricketing fan.

What does this mean? Well it means that to be a professional batsman or bowler the elite athlete must possess what it takes to succedd at both formats of the game and be able to make necessary adjustments to his technique and mental approach in order to switch between what we call oneday and test cricket mode. Each has its unique demands on batters and bowlers and the professional cricketer, if he is serious about his spot in the side, in one way makes a pledge and oath to be able to effectively adjust the mental and technical adjustment required such that he can succeed, satisfy the fansd and ultimately not let mental toughness to let their full ability and full talent down.

There is a big difference between preparing, training for and contesting a game of cricket across the two formats and in a sense the professional cricketer is training for two entirely different sports or ball games, so to speak! The professional cricketer, and one who will not only do what he can to help the team win, but protect his reputation as an elite athlete is suddenly under intense pressure to practice hard **AND** smart in order to protect his reputation as a professional cricketer per say.

If an elite cricketer does not do this he is not only not going to be worthy of professional athlete and professional cricketer status, but will struggle to produce consistent performances across both formats and find it extremely difficult to rise the ranks of district, club and domestic level cricket and go on to become a professional and play for the country. There are a few key or main qualities or elements which the professional batsman or bowler **MUST** be weary of and pay particular attention to if he is to competently handle the demands of the particular format he is playing and contesting at the time. These adjustments which the professional batsman **MUST** make are listed below:

- Adjustment of backlift and playing in the 'V'
- Adjustment of visual method – primary vs peripheral vision
- Adjusting the getting a sighter period and its length
- Playing multiple shots to the same delivery – negotiating the c-box
- Being more liberal or conservative in regards offering shots to the semi loose ball
- Picking the line the *'sequential'* method **OR** the *'Parallel method'*
- Playing according to an inccreased or decreased sized z-box
- Playing orthodox percentage cricket vs improvised and attacking cricket

This is what the professional batsman is up against if he is to succeed at both formats of the game and make a career out of cricket and be classed in the *'professional category'*. We will now in turn look at each key requirement or demand the professional batsman must attain competency in one by one and discuss them in a little detail such that you know the what and why on a more intricate level.

Adjustment of backlift and playing in the 'V':

This aspect to batting allows us to play safe percentage cricket especially early in the innings and not let the good accurate ball lead to your demise. Because the ball invariably swings in elite cricket in both formats, it is theorised that you should bring your backlift down dead straight and follow through dead straight and endeavour to only play straight and in the 'V' and focus on the vertical bat shots more than the cross bat shots. Usually we straighten our backlift and play in the 'V' as a bread and butter routine within test cricket predominantly as we are trying to get ourselves set, played in and used to the bowling and pitch and go on to make a century, however if a batter is playing say a 50 over game and team absolutely needs him to stay at the crease and make a score, then this approach can be and **IS** warranted in oneday cricket also. The reason we straighten our backlift and play in the 'V' early on is so that we can get a sighter and not get out cheaply to the accurate ball early on or play an impetuous or risky shot when our wicket is valuable for the team's sake of winning. Similarly, in oneday cricket it is theorised that we play with a backlift coming more from 2nd or 3rd slip such that we can get more batspeed and power in our shots as well as play the horizontal bat shots with more power and conviction. So these two theories must be considered by the professional batter while he is playing elite level cricket especially the deploying of a dead straight backlift and playing in the 'V' early on and he must be swift in regard to how is going to tackle or approach the bowling – with a straight back-lift or a more rounded one or only play straight or also play across the line.[25]

Adjustment of visual method – primary vs peripheral vision:
In both formats of the game we generally always keep our primary vision open for the good length accurate ball and peripheral vision open to the attacking stroke, however it is just the duration we do this across the two formats which varies. In oneday cricket we might do this for only 4-7 balls and in Test cricket we might do this for a good 3-4 overs. It is upto the batsman and how comfortable he is with picking the length and seeing the ball early which dictates how many balls we do this for or even whether we do it at all – in 20-20 cricket we may leave our primary vision open to the attacking stroke and only the peripheral vision open to the defensive stroke. It all depends on the format the batter is playing and how comfortable he is with the bowler's pattern and how the pitch is playing.[26]

Adjusting the getting a sighter period and its length:
Usually, just to be safe and guarantee a score, in test cricket we give ourselves a longer time to get a sighter and try do so more accurately. That is, gauge in a more precise, accurate and meticulous manner where exactly the z-box lies, what is a good length and what is not **AND** especially what is at a driveable

---

[25] In either format of the game it is a general rule that even in oneday cricket we deploy a dead straight backlift and play only in the 'V' at least for 4-7 balls!

[26] If the batter is super confident with his ability to negotiate the accurate ball and one which may swing then he can from the ball 1 start playing in one day mode – which is to leave the primary vision open to the attacking stroke.

length and what is not! In oneday cricket the pressure is on to get as bigger score as possible and keep up with the ensuing run-rate pressures at the time and we are under pressure to not waste any time by taking too long to start playing good attacking and forceful cricket, and this is when we restrict ourselves to a sighter period of say 3-6 balls.

Playing multiple shots to the same delivery – negotiating the c-box:

This is perhaps the biggest and most crucial aspect to attaining a professional batsman status – the c-box that is! In Test cricket we aim to play that one particular shot which is considered the most orthodox and classical shot to that particular line and length and focus on playing an orthodox classical style of batsmanship; whereas in one day cricket we must have the aptness, dexterity and brashness to play any one of a possible 3-5 shots to any particular delivery. This is also one of the key attributes the professional batsman must posses and be apt in if he is to succeed at both formats of the game and attain proffessional status.

Being more liberal or conservative in regards offering shots to the semi loose ball:

In Test cricket if a ball is only marginally loose we treat it as a good ball and play defense; however, in oneday cricket because we are in attacking mode we treat even the semi loose ball as loose and try play a scoring shot. For example if the ball lands on the fringe of the z-box we then decide to be either more conservative and play safe or conversely we might aim to be more daring and brash and play a big scoring shot from it.

Picking the line the *'sequential'* method OR the *'Parallel method'*:

As you now know there are 2 methods of picking line. One where we pick and react to line earlier and one where we pick and react to line later. It is all tied up with what stage of your innings you are in **AND** whether you playing oneday or Test cricket. At the start of your innings **ALWAYS** pick line the *'sequential'* method and as you get a feel for how much lateral ways movement or swing the bowler is getting slowly beging to pick and react to the line the *'parallel'* method. If you are in a hurry to get runs at a faster run-rate, as is the case in oneday cricket, then you might choose to pick the line the parallel method. [27]

Playing according to an increased or decreased sized z-box:

Usually only in oneday cricket we deccrease the size of our z-box and subsequently increase our c-box and array of shots we can ultimately offer, however, even in Test cricket it is perfectly possible and has been done players like Viv Richards, Tendulkar and Sehwag to play to a decreased sized z-box even whilst batting in test cricket. Generally, stick to the standard z-box and outer z-box in Test cricket and leave playing to an inner sized z-box only for whilst batting in oneday cricket, however as we said if you are confident enough and seeing the ball like a football then there's no reason why you cant play oneday cricket even in a test match! [28]

---

[27] You may also choose to pick line in parallel even in test cricket just like many top players can do. It all depends on your confidence in adjusting your bodily movement late if the ball does swing.

[28] Virender Sehwag & Viv Richards are the 2 best examples of the ability to play to a decreased sized z-box even in Test cricket. It all depends how good your eye is!

Playing orthodox percentage cricket vs improvised and attacking cricket:

It is imperative we play good orthodox and percentage cricket in test matches so that we don't all get out to the good accurate ball and collapse for a meagre total. Similarly, it is so imperative that once we get settled and our 'eye-in' that we start treating our c-box with maximum vigour and in the most optimal manner possible via improvising and 'thinking outside of the box' as opposed to just playing your stock standard orthodox shot you would play in test cricket. That is, in one day cricket it is important that you not get tied down and let the run-rate dip due to certain field placings and tactics deployed by the bowler to restrict your scoring. You do this by having 3-5 different shots you can successfully execute to the same ball in order to find the gap in the field. [29]

---

[29] Note, sometimes even in test cricket the bowling side might have you tied down and get on top of you making it important for you to be able to play 3-5 shots to the same ball – just like you would in oneday cricket.

A NOTE BY THE AUTHOR:

Consider this book as the bare bones and skeleton of the full coaching and educational experience we *'PhD cricket'* are here to offer you. This book is only intended to awaken your conscious mind as to the various intricacies which exist in cricket and not so much to actually teach you how to acquire them – the key skills relevant to cricket and how to acquire them are provided within the other specialised manuals. We are merely trying to get your cricketing brain switched on for the more advanced and deeper lessons which lie within the core sequence of specialized coaching manuals we have devised on the game – a game considered the great mental sport and one which **CANNOT** be mastered without a little study and intellectual understanding!

It must be remembered and acknowledged by the aspiring cricketer that cricket chooses **YOU** and not **YOU** choose cricket. You must build and grow your game sufficient enough to catch the selector's eyes and have something to offer the national team. This will take hard work and pracctice but most importantly a deeper understanding of the game on a scientific and technical level. Cricket being the great mental sport and acknowledged worldwide as being 70% - 90% mental and won in the mind, it is that mental spark and scientific rigor and approach to the game which is going to catch the selector's eyes and we, through the writing of our 9 specialised coaching manuals, are here to give to you this mental spark which is going to make or break your hopes of becoming a professional and playing for the country!

The point of this book is to make you knowledgeable in the what and why and not so much the how, and is designed so that you get a full picture of what cricket is about and the hidden science which must be understood in order to play for the country, and also to make you appreciate the fact that the understanding of vector forces is necessary for both batter, bowler, fielder and captain.

So just so you know what you're up against and what you are getting yourself into can be considered the main purpose or theme of the book. It is relatively brief and we have kept it to the point as much as possible, as there is more reading ahead of you if you are to develop the confidence it takes to play for the country. Many intricate details about cricket have not been discussed and depicted in this book as we only want to give you a condensed and brief acquaintance regarding the vitalities and essential or critical aspects of cricket you **MUST** master to aim for national selection and not bombard you with the complete and entire picture just yet. The remaining knowledge and expertise which PhD cricket is here to teach you to the finest of detail lies within our other specialized manuals where an entire book is devoted to teach a particular topic or sets of topics regarding batting and spin bowling.

Take this book as only an introduction and the starting point of your journey of being coached, guided and mentored in the most thorough and profound way and the beginning of the rigorous journey ahead you are about to embark upon – being selected for your country.

Like our videos say, we are here to look after you for a lifetime and you need not look elsewhere to find your lessons about cricket. *'PhD cricket'* is officially on the scene and if you read and follow onto our books you are guaranteed to reach your full potential as a cricketer within weeks or days and possibly even overnight – this is our guarantee!

PhD cricket is officially on the scene and we have big plans for you. Plans of transforming potential and talent into real results and achievements on the cricket field. We take the onus upon our shoulders to give you the revelations and impetus to perfect your technique and game and achieve results and all you need do is read word for word and follow on – we have done all the hard work of *'nutting'* out the science for you as well as conveying this science in the most meticulous yet concise and user friendly manner possible.

Acquire our books on batting and spin bowling in your custody immediately and get busy reading, for each day playing your game the uninformed and uneducated way is doing harm and is to the detriment of you gaining national selection in a sport which is supremely competitive and played at a serious level by millions of boys and girls around the world.

You need not be worried we are wasting your time because we are **NOT** and we have given you a money back guarantee to prove that we are not, so acquire the other books in your custody immediately and get reading and rise the ranks fast and do justice to your talent. Cricket is a competitive sport and you must act fast!

All the best in a brighter cricketing journey ahead. We are 100% certain that our books will give you exactly what you need to fulfil your dreams of playing for the state or country.

All the best in a successful cricketing journey ahead,

Sincerely,

Nikhil Jain

(Specialist side-on & front-on off spinner, slow leg spinner & medium pace leg spinner and opening batsman for ACT Australian state level cricket, 1992-1996)

www.ingramcontent.com/pod-product-compliance
Lightning Source LLC
LaVergne TN
LVHW041848070526
838199LV00045BA/1495